EVERYONE IS AFRAID

ISBN: 979-8-9889566-1-7

EVERYONE IS AFRAID

A FABLE OF FEAR, FRIENDSHIP, AND FLOURISHING

RON MACKLIN

MacklinConnection

To Koni, my love.

CONTENTS

FOREWORD
by Bowen White, a.k.a. Dr Jerko

As a high school freshman I had a girlfriend named Sue. Everything was great until my birthday. She gave me a card which, upon reading, gave me no choice but to break up with her. I didn't know why at the time, I just knew it had to be done. I figured it out much later. She used the L word.

Virginia Satir, famous family therapist, said our ability to make choices is directly related to self esteem.

When I read the "I love you" message, my poor self esteem gave me no choice. She was getting too close and that kind of intimacy was too risky. Sound it out. Intimacy – InToMeSee…... She might discover the truth. I wasn't really worth her affection.

I pushed her away to stay safe and secure behind the mask I wore to trick her into liking me. And I broke up with her not because of how I felt about her, but because of how I felt about me! That is an example of how our treatment of those with whom we are in relationship is determined, more by feelings for self than our feelings for the other. And the reverse is also true.

How others treat you is much more about *them* than it is about *you*.

Seeing Sue years later, we had a short visit. I told her the reason I'd come to understand and she understood immediately. I couldn't put a name to it then, but I can now. It's related to our best kept secret and what this book is about.

There are two related issues that I would like to explore here before you read the story that follows.

Number one has to do with our best kept secret. Number two has to do with the fact that science alone can take us only so far down the path toward what is a healthy, heartfelt life well lived.

Let's start with number two. What is the number one killer disease here in western civilization?

Coronary Artery Disease, i.e., heart disease. The clogged arteries that feed the heart, studied thoroughly for decades prove positive lifestyle health habits can delay its onset.

However, another more recent important discovery shows the healthy support of a group of people is also protective against heart disease.

The other heart ailment that can be fatal is electrical and is addressed in public health announcements.

The heart transmits an electrical impulse coordinating its musculature. If it's disrupted, it can create an abnormal rhythm and stops pumping blood out into the great vessels that feed the brain and rest of the body. The result can be cardiac arrest....unless CPR, cardiopulmonary resuscitation, is quickly administered.

We actually have two hearts. I know, that's not scientific, but it's true. The one above is physical and is related to but separate from our second, non physical...metaphorical heart. It's the one we open when we fall in love or hold our newborn. The one poets and spiritual leaders have spoken of and is felt when spending time with special friends as depicted in the story to follow.

However, our best kept secret can get in the way of making great connections with others, (e.g., Sue and I) and having those close personal relationships which allow us to give and receive healthy support. Nonetheless, with awareness of this part of us, we can keep it from running the engine of the psyche and driving our behavior and mood. So, what is this secret?

Consider child development. All children hear and do learn there is only one way of doing things, that's "the right way." And children learn what that "right way" is by traveling the final common pathway of learning. That is through trial and error.

In other words, we earn our learning by trying again and again until we finally get it right. And when each mistake is made, warmth is withheld eliciting a cold parental retort reinforcing our feelings of inadequacy.

"Bad boy" "What's wrong with you?"

"You should be ashamed of yourself?"

"If I've told you once, I've told you a thousand times..."

We all got our feelings of inadequacy reinforced over and over. However, when we've done it wrong enough times, we did learn "right way" behaviors.

Then, performance criteria being met, we received parental warmth with positive feedback: "We're very proud of you." (once)

You do the math. It shows, we all got more specific negative feedback than positive on the "right way" roads we've traveled on the way to grownup.

And getting our feelings of inadequacy reinforced so often, we grew a part of us that stays with us throughout our lives. That's our best kept secret. We all have that part of us with those feelings of inadequacy which I've named the Scared One. And the Scared One resides within the psyche, is related to the ego and never goes away.

Why not?

The voice of the parent becomes the inner voice of the child who is the father of the man. So as grownups, when we make a mistake, we don't need anyone else to reinforce our feelings of inadequacy. Why not? "I'd rather do it myself!" And, sadly we do.

Carl Jung said we act out on the world stage what is unresolved within the psyche. The Scared One is acting out our lives unbeknownst to us while unconsciously compensating for feelings of inadequacy. We can therefore be ambitiously driven to be successful as psychic compensation for feelings of inadequacy.

"If I could just get that promotion......then." But no matter what we achieve, there is no critical mass of fame and/or money that will send the Scared One packing.

The Scared One is driven by the fear that at any moment we could be exposed as inadequate. Since fear is the driver of the stress response, which is a survival response, we can't let down our guard. We have to be constantly vigilant which means chronically stressed. Whew!!

Unless.....unless we become conscious of that part of us and take the wheel of the psyche, tell the Scared One to get in the back seat and consciously apply the brake. Whoa.......I need a walk, some fresh air, drink of water and to talk with a friend. I need some healthy support. Or, get this, a friend gets ahold of you and has an issue troubling them and could use another set of eyes and ears on their issue. We need each other but the Scared One doesn't want to admit it. Yet the problems we have call forth the gifts of others just as their problems call forth our gifts. And in that way we can participate meaningfully in the lives of each other.

However, if the Scared One is running the show, being vulnerable and asking for help is a no no. So we have to act in spite of our fear. It takes courage to let down our guard and ask for what we need by being vulnerable. It's funny because the Scared One's motto is safety and security at all costs. Well guess where that safety and security rests? It resides in our close personal relationships with friends who won't take advantage of our vulnerability. Not by cowering alone behind our shields which I did by pushing Sue away from me.

The Latin root for ambition is the verb *ambire* and originally referred to soliciting for votes by building esteem in the eyes of voters. What we're talking about here is electing yourself *in spite of* your feelings of inadequacy. Because you have them doesn't mean you're inadequate. By the time we've grown up, we have mastered so many behaviors and know how to do so many things well, we become the people we used to complain about.

That is parents, leaders, teachers, coaches, business owners, lawyers, etc., all productive members of the community.

Turns out, friendship is the best medicine. Befriend yourself first and you'll be a better friend, parent and partner, etc.

It's a positive health habit! The over 80 year long Harvard Grant Study shows that when your metaphorical heart gets out of rhythm, it needs CPR too.

Close Personal Relationships (CPR) enhance wellbeing, health, happiness, financial success and longevity more than genes or intelligence.

It's our turn. Forget perfect. Value, esteem yourself as is, flaws and all. That's self esteem. Who would benefit? You would and everyone in your relational orbit.

Introduction

RON'S WHYS

Why title a book *Everyone Is Afraid*? I'll get to that before I complete the introduction.

My memories of growing up include receiving books from my Grandpa, normally with a brief note inside the front cover: "To Ronny from your Grandpa Lorin, 1969." The warmest memory is of sitting on the couch, leaning against him and listening as he read to me. I felt safe next to this rough farmer who grew up riding a horse to school. As I listened to him read *Wilderness Champion*, *Little House on the Prairie*, and *The Call of the Wild*, I fell in love with stories—stories about challenges, suffering, struggling, winning and losing, journeying, hunting, being hunted, living off the land, adventures, and fun. Fun is an interesting word. The *Oxford English Dictionary* says it means enjoyment, amusement, or lighthearted pleasure. From the couch, leaning against Grandpa, I would have called that the meaning of boring! Fun is when I don't know the outcome, when I struggle, get help, make lots of mistakes, create new ideas, and watch stuff go badly. Because in the end we create something that satisfies us all more than we thought possible.

I guess that's why my mother put a poster in my bedroom that said: "The greatest pleasure in life is doing what others say can't be done." When I began writing this book, the person saying it couldn't be done was me. I love stories and *despise* writing. I studied engineering because it had the least amount of English required. Well, that and I remember someone saying I wasn't a good enough student. Grrr! But I'm also the person who took that poster's message to heart. So, here's the book from the guy who says he despises writing.

Now for the title. In 1997 I was thirty-two and had recently finished my Executive MBA at Rockhurst University. Several people had said I couldn't do it, but that's another story. I somehow finagled an invitation to an executive morning meeting featuring Dr. Bowen White. I got there early and sat in the front of the room, as if being closer would allow me to learn more. When I looked around, I realized I was the youngest, least experienced person in the room. So I made up a quick story: I did not belong in the room.

This clown walked in—really a clown. Big bum, big shoes, red nose, wearing a lab coat. He introduced himself as Dr. Yurko, spelled Jerko. He started talking about executive performance, fear, and not believing you're enough. Dr. Jerko asked this question: "How many of you are afraid and think there is something wrong with you because you are afraid? Raise your hand."

I remember feeling my heart pounding. I wanted to hide, to run out of the room. Writing this now has caused all the emotions to flood back in. I was sitting at the front table facing him, and I felt he was going to point at me and say, "Here he is! Someone escort him out of the room." I surrendered to that idea. As I was raising my hand, Dr. Jerko began to raise his hand to point at me. I felt like a fraud. I had no right to be in that room that day.

But as Dr. Jerko's finger singled me out, he quietly said, "Look around." I did not want to look around. I thought holding my hand up to admit I was afraid and that there was something wrong with me required all the courage I had. Again, I surrendered. But I began to turn and look around. In this room full of successful executives from all over the Kansas City area, every hand was raised.

If I could have remembered how to cry, I would have. My whole nervous system was suddenly alive and peaceful at the same time. I had a new story: everyone is afraid, and it's human to be afraid.

The book you are about to read is a fable. I chose the fable format because I learn more from stories. That's because I get lost in the tale and all my shields drop. Shields are stories in our heads that protect us. They protect us from things we don't understand and from beliefs we created when we were five, nine, fifteen, thirty, or even forty-five years old. These stories made sense at the time, and we forget that we made them up. They seem real. So we're not open to learning something different.

How could we be open? We already have everything figured out. But when I'm reading, listening to, or watching a story, I forget my shields. Then the learning can sneak in before I know it.

When I'm in the middle of a story and I can relate to the characters, learning drifts in and kind of dwells for a time. Then later I think, "Whoa, where did that come from?" Whatever the idea is, I find it came from a story I read, watched, or listened to days or weeks before. Maybe this happens because our ancestors sat around the cooking fire telling stories for a hundred thousand years, sharing tales of great successes, great failures, hunts and being hunted, loves and losses, and what tomorrow or next season might bring.

In this story you will meet Alex, Sheri, Lucy, Steve, Teddy, Julie, Harriet, Jim, Todd, Bhavani, Desiree, Evi, Peter, Judy, Fred, and Harry. Their characters and situations come from the last fifty years of my life. Their stories are based on my own and on those of all the people I have had vulnerable conversations with. If you notice yourself in this book—things you regret doing or not doing, events you kept from others, times when you closed yourself off—you are not alone. I have the same stories, or my version of the same stories.

I'll see you on the other side of the story.

Chapter 1:

GHOSTS FROM THE PAST

Alex's route was predictable. Every morning he rode the train to Van Buren station and then made his way to the 200 block of Michigan Avenue. The South Loop was more his home than his actual home because he spent more time there, in his office, seven stories up.

His path was worked out almost to the minute. He always arrived earlier than anyone else at the Conner, Conner, and Moore law firm, and he often left after most everyone had gone. His father had drilled a work ethic into his head from an early age. "Alex, to be on time is to be early," he would say.

Because it was a Monday morning in February, the streets were full of dirty snow, and the wind blowing off Lake Michigan was brutal. Alex always picked up a copy of the *Tribune* from Harry's Newsstand on his way in. Harry always said hello, but

Alex never acknowledged him with anything but a grunt as he handed him the money for the paper. Alex could easily have the paper delivered to his door, but he was a creature of routine. Harry's took him three minutes.

Next, he would stop in Harriet's Bean Emporium. Harriet always had Alex's drink ready when he came in because his order was always the same: a cappuccino with an extra shot, double foam. Alex paid with exact change, a dollar for a tip. Six minutes.

Then he would walk across the street to his office building, use his key card to get in, go to the seventh floor, and flip on his computer—seven minutes total. Perfect timing, every day. Alex never allowed anything to distract him from his routine. There was comfort in the predictable, and he hoped his diligence would be noticed. For eight years, he'd been working as an associate corporate attorney for Conner, Conner, and Moore. He had brought them three big clients, yet he still had not been offered a junior partner position. Some people who had only been with the firm for five years were not only junior partners but were being groomed for senior partnership. When Alex asked why he was being passed over, the answers from the partners were vague, and he often felt uncomfortable. Alex decided he wasn't working hard enough; they would have to notice if he put in the hours.

The previous month, he'd begun working to bring a multibillion-dollar pharmaceutical company in as a client. He'd just started meeting with them, and the firm had noticed and added some of their top attorneys to help seal the deal. This made Alex uncomfortable, as he thought others would take credit for his work, so he doubled down. He was supposed to take a week's

EVERYONE IS AFRAID

vacation in Florida to escape the cold of the Midwest for spring break, but he canceled it. His wife, Sheri, was not happy about it, nor were his children. They had been planning the family vacation for months, and he had given them the bad news at the last minute. But this deal was too important; it could be his ticket to partnership. Alex's father had become a junior partner in just four years, and Alex had seen the disappointment in his eyes when his parents visited him last.

Replaying last night's argument with his wife, Alex stepped off the train. She failed to see how important this deal was and how they could take trips to France or Italy rather than Disney World when he became a partner. He remembered hearing about a podcast that discussed money and health. He thought it could be good to listen to something on the train ride home instead of worrying about everything. Maybe it would allow some distraction. He committed to finding it during lunchtime.

The platform was crowded as Alex made his way out of the station and onto Michigan Ave. He looked at his watch, and he was two minutes behind schedule. Perhaps he needed to skip the paper this morning and pick one up at lunch. As he walked out, he passed a man huddling for warmth and holding a cardboard sign: "Out of work. Anything helps." Alex had made it a rule not to make eye contact with any homeless that occupied downtown Chicago's streets. It wasn't that he wasn't generous, as he gave to office charities quite often. He felt the homeless were often addicts and that whatever he might give them would only fund their next score.

But Alex broke his own rule and looked at the man. In that brief moment, as the bustle around him seemed to freeze in time,

Alex recognized the face, and his heart skipped a beat. He quickly looked away in case the man might recognize him. Then Alex blew past Harry's Newsstand and neglected to stop at Harriet's Bean Emporium, even though his daily cup was probably waiting for him, with "Alex" scrawled on the side. By the time he reached the office, the trek was a blur.

"It can't be him. It just can't be," Alex said to himself in the empty office. Perhaps he needed a break. After getting home in the evenings, he'd keep working until his eyes closed on their own. Now his tired eyes were playing tricks on him. Alex went through his day distracted, thinking about the man at the train station.

During lunch he remembered that he wanted something to distract him during the train ride home. He found the *WealthyWellthy* podcast and started scrolling through episodes. "Everything Is an Adventure" stood out. The thought of adventure seemed good. He silenced his phone to allow focused work for the afternoon.

The sound of a vacuum broke him out of his zone; it was time to go home. All the offices were dark. He walked past the woman dumping the contents of his trash can into her cart. What was her name? She had told him once, but he had forgotten it.

As he walked to the train station, his heart pumped faster. What if he was still there? What if it really was his old friend from college? It didn't seem possible. The man he had seen that morning was diminished, his face gaunt. The smile Alex had seen so many times on his friend's face couldn't fit on the sad, gray one he had beheld earlier. But what if it was his old friend? What would he say? Would he pass him by and not say anything?

The area around the train station entrance was clear, which was a blessing because it was double digits below zero outside. Alex stepped on the train, confused and conflicted. There was a big meeting with a potential new client in three days, and he had lots of work to do.

He put in earbuds, turned on the noise-canceling feature, and set his watch to time the thirty-five-minute train ride. Then he started "Everything Is an Adventure."

•　•　•　•　•　•

The house was quiet when Alex arrived home, which was unusual. Sheri was typically wrangling the kids while finishing dinner, but most of the lights were out. There was no Sheri, Steve, or Lucy. In the kitchen was a note:

> *Alex,*
> *The kids and I are at Mom's. They wanted to visit as we haven't been over there in weeks. I'll get them to school in the morning. There is some meatloaf in the fridge to heat up. I'll see you tomorrow night.*
> *Love, Sheri*

That was odd. Sheri would usually call. Alex looked at his phone. Seven missed calls! He remembered turning on the Do Not Disturb function after lunch. He'd had meetings all afternoon and had forgotten to turn it off. He called Sheri's phone and only got voice mail. Maybe it was a blessing, as he would have a quiet house for the evening to prepare for the Friday meeting.

As Alex ate his dinner, the homeless man's eyes were burning in his mind. There was hopelessness in there, and it turned Alex's stomach. He scraped the remainder of his dinner into the trash, went to his home office, and worked late into the night.

Chapter 2:

RECONNECTING WITH AN OLD FRIEND

Alex was nervous—his routine was off. He'd had a restless night and had slept through the alarm. This was not like Alex at all. He rushed to shower and get out the door, looking at his watch a dozen times. This was not the time to slack off, not with a big account coming in. Alex had to be his best; too much was on the line. The partners were watching, and this was his one chance to impress them.

As he rode the train, he could not stop thinking about Teddy. It had been what? At least ten years since they'd talked? Or maybe it had been more; Alex couldn't be sure. Teddy was one of the first people he'd met at the University of Northern Iowa. Even though Teddy was a freshman, he'd walked around campus like he'd been there for years. Alex marveled at his confidence. They lived next door to one another and hit it off immediately.

Alex came from a middle-class farming family in Nebraska, but Teddy came from old money. His family was worth millions. That was one of the things Alex was trying to wrap his head around. Teddy was a software genius and had family money to fall back on. So how in the world could it be the same man he had seen the day before begging for change? It just didn't make any sense. The more Alex thought about it, the more convinced he was that the man wasn't Teddy. After all, how could he be sure this was what Teddy looked like now? The man at the station had a definite resemblance to Teddy, but he was gaunt and had a gray pallor to his skin. Teddy was so vain in college that there was no way he would let himself go like that unless something was seriously wrong.

Alex tried to force his mind to consider all he needed to do in the next week to prepare for the new client. He and some of the partners were due to meet with the C-level executives to work out the details by early next week. A final date couldn't be set until the executives had read and digested the proposal, so Alex needed to complete it in the next couple of days.

The doors opened, and Alex stepped off the train. He looked at the ground as he exited the car and made his way out of the station. He didn't want to look up and see his friend because he was unsure how to handle it.

The weather had cleared a bit, but the wind cut through Alex's clothes. It was called the Windy City for a reason, but the icy cold made it worse. Alex stopped to adjust his scarf and zip up his jacket. He picked up his bag, and when he looked up, Teddy stood before him, staring with sunken eyes.

"Al . . . Alex?" stuttered Teddy. "Oh my God, it *is* you! I thought I saw you yesterday, but you vanished in the morning mob."

Alex's stomach tightened, and the frigid air seemed to suffocate him. It *was* Teddy. Alex wanted to run past his morning coffee and paper and go straight to his office so he could hide under his desk. He felt a lump form in his throat. He cleared it a couple of times before he could find his voice.

"Teddy?" he finally croaked. "Hey . . . Teddy . . . How are you, man? What's going on?"

Alex could see Teddy's eyes well up, and he felt terrible. He put down his case, opened his arms, and embraced Teddy. Alex felt like he was holding bones rather than hugging his old friend.

"Come on," said Alex. "Let's get out of the cold and have some coffee."

"I'd like that," replied Teddy in a choked voice. Alex could tell the man was trying his hardest not to break down, and it made him want to cry as well.

. . . . . .

Because Alex was late, his morning coffee was not in its regular spot on the counter at Harriet's Bean Emporium.

"Oh, Alex," said Harriet as she steamed some milk for a coffee. "I didn't think you were coming."

"That's OK," Alex said. "I'll have my regular in a real coffee mug this morning, and my friend will have a half-caf soy latte with sugar-free caramel." He turned and looked at Teddy. "Right?"

"I can't believe you remembered," said Teddy. "I really don't have any . . ." He began counting his change from the morning's donations.

"Teddy. This is on me. Are you hungry? Harriet makes some of the best breakfast sandwiches in Chicago—chorizo, gouda, fried egg on a ciabatta roll."

"That sounds great," said Teddy, looking at the floor. "I'll pay you back when—"

"Stop it already," Alex insisted. "Two breakfast sandwiches as well, Harriet."

Harriet didn't blink at the man in torn clothes and a jacket that barely fit him. She only smiled.

Alex and Teddy sat in the back of the shop, and the heat from the overhead vent warmed them quickly.

"It is so good to see you, Alex," said Teddy as he blew on his coffee. "By the looks of your suit and Italian loafers, it seems like you reached your goal of becoming a partner at a firm."

"Well, not quite yet," Alex admitted. "I'm really close, but you know what they say—you have to dress for success, right?"

There was an awkward silence. Harriet brought the sandwiches and an extra chocolate croissant, which she placed in front of Teddy. "This is something a little extra from me," she said in her friendly Jamaican accent. "If you can't eat it now, I'll bag it up for you and have a coffee for you to go."

"Thank you so much," said Teddy with a smile.

"Anything for a friend of Alex's," replied Harriet. "He's a

favorite customer of mine, even though he is always rushing here and there. He never has time to stay and enjoy Harriet's coffee. It's good to see him sit and enjoy a cup." She winked and walked back to the counter to pull more coffee and fill more orders.

Teddy gently and methodically unwrapped the foil around the sandwich, took a small bite, and chewed. "You're right," he said. "This is delicious." But he put the sandwich down and looked at the table.

Alex didn't have much of an appetite either. He looked at his watch. People would start filling the offices in the next fifteen minutes. He didn't want to cut his friend short, but he didn't want to be late. What would the partners think about tardiness when so much still needed to be completed?

"Teddy," Alex began. "I'm glad to see you, but I can't stay long."

Teddy stood up quickly, almost spilling his coffee. "Oh, course. I am so sorry. I didn't mean to take up your time. I know you must be busy."

"No, no, please sit down," Alex said with a sigh. "It's been a long time since we've talked. I can take the time. Can you tell me what's happened?"

"Well, I uh . . ." Teddy mumbled.

"I don't want to pry. Maybe we could talk."

"You're OK," said Teddy. "It's just a long story, and I'm a bit embarrassed that you're seeing me like this."

Alex nodded and took out his phone. He typed a quick message to his assistant saying he would be late and asking if he could begin editing the proposal on the shared drive.

The response was quick: *Of course, I'll get right on it.*

"Don't be embarrassed, Teddy," Alex said, putting his phone away. "I know we haven't talked in a long time, but I still consider you my friend. I want to be able to help if I can." Alex was surprised to hear the words come out of his mouth. Sure, he would like to help Teddy, but he didn't really have the time right now. Maybe he could give him some money or call a family member to help him. Teddy looked like he was in bad shape. Alex had expected his friend to gobble down the sandwich, but he had only taken one bite, barely large enough to feed a mouse. He was gaunt, and his skin looked a little too tight around his cheekbones. What had become of his friend?

"I appreciate that, Alex, more than you can know. I know you're busy, so maybe some other time."

"No, really, Teddy. I already told my office I'll be coming in later, so I have the time. And there are no judgments here, trust me."

Again, where were these words coming from? Of course he was judging him. Out of their friend group, Teddy had clearly been the one most likely to succeed. Alex wondered if he had committed some crime or maybe violated some securities laws and lost everything to the government. Whatever it was, it must be bad. He wasn't sure how he could help his old friend, but for now, he could at least lend an ear.

"Oh, OK. Can I have some water? I'm enjoying the coffee, but it's a little hard on my stomach," said Teddy.

"Of course." Alex looked toward the counter. "Harriet, can you bring some water, please?"

"Coming right up," Harriet replied cheerfully.

After she'd placed a glass in front of Teddy, he took a few sips and then paused. "Other than my family, I haven't told this to anyone. A lot has happened, and sometimes my brain gets messed up, so please be patient. I'll try to tell this the best I can. I guess I'll start at the point you last saw me."

EVERYONE IS AFRAID

Chapter 3:

TEDDY'S TALE

After college, I traveled a bit around Europe on Dad's dime. In Germany, I met a girl named Julie, who was traveling abroad to study art. She was beautiful and brilliant—a deadly combination. The crazy thing was that she was into me too. We had this whirlwind romance in Berlin. We flew back to Vegas for a week, and we got married.

Even though she was American as well, she didn't tell her family she was back or getting married. Her parents were cool with it. They were a couple of leftover hippies and were just excited she found me. My parents, on the other hand, were pissed. Dad told me since I was now a man, I needed to get a job and support a family. Julie and I settled near Chicago. She still had a year left in school, so I began sending my résumé around, and this up-and-coming tech company, Nu-Horizon, hired me to help them with a project. They weren't quite up and fully running, so it was supposed to be for just one project. The pay was crap, but I was getting some real-life experience.

Between Julie's student loans and my meager salary, we could only rent a cheap one-bedroom apartment. It wasn't much, but we were happy. So happy about those first years. Eventually, Julie graduated, and soon after, we had our daughter, Hannah. We decided that Julie would hold off on her career to care for Hannah.

This worked out great since the software I had been working on became a moneymaker for Nu-Horizon, and they were able to hire me full time as their developer. The company grew by leaps and bounds, as did my workload. I spent more time at the office than at home, and we never had time for a vacation. Most holidays were half days, and I'd return to the office after opening presents or having a family meal.

Within a year, we had Dillon, but Julie was becoming increasingly agitated about my work schedule. It wasn't just that I wasn't around; she wanted to work on her career. Someone she knew from college had offered her a position in a large gallery. We hired a nanny for the kids so she could work nights at the gallery. We were passing ships, and the distance between us grew. I was just too distracted to notice it.

This went on for a few more years, and in my head, everything was fine. We were living in a nicer house and in a trendy neighborhood. There was a neighborhood swimming pool for the kids, and the schools in the area were some of the best in the state. We had new cars and the best clothes, and to me, we were living the dream life.

It was my dream, not Julie's. We argued more and more. She said we weren't a family. I told her that I would take some time for a real vacation. We were growing the company, but my new position as the head of development would mean a change in responsibilities. I would have more time for her and the kids. At least, that's what I was telling myself. I even convinced myself that I would have time for friends, and I intended to reach out to you and the others in our little group. I wanted to see all of our crew, but that never happened either.

Fast-forward to about two years ago. A larger company offered to buy out Nu-Horizon. There was a lot of excitement, and the company's founders were in a position to make a lot of money. I had never considered what a merger could mean for me. I thought it would mean a larger salary and better benefits. It never occurred to me that I could be without a job. The merger went through, and I was given three months to help transition the people taking over my department. Then I was let go. I was dumbfounded and lost.

This was also the end of Julie and me. It wasn't because I lost my income; it was because I withdrew from her and our family. The burden to save my marriage was on me, and I didn't want anyone's help. The problem was, I didn't recognize the problem. I didn't understand that my unwillingness to talk with my wife and spend more time with my children was the issue.

Julie suggested we go to counseling, but I refused. I didn't believe a stranger could help, and even if they could, there was no big problem in the first place. I felt Julie needed to be more understanding and give me more space. I didn't see that withdrawing from her and the kids was what was breaking us apart.

My position was that I was the man of the family. The prince, the protector, the provider, and the problem solver. But as the weeks rolled by with no job prospects, I fell into depression and despair. Instead of facing my problems and seeking help, I blamed Julie for everything I felt was wrong with our family. I told her she needed to contribute more, clean more, and be more attentive. I refused to see that *she* was the glue holding everything together and that I needed to support her, not make her life harder.

Everyone has their breaking point, and ours occurred in the kitchen. I yelled at her for not putting the plates in the dishwasher correctly. She snapped and took the plates out and then dropped them on the floor. They shattered everywhere.

It was at that moment I knew the problem was me, but I was so ashamed I froze.

"Is this better?" she said. "Maybe you should do the dishes yourself from now on."

There was not enough groveling in the world to get her to stay.

She decided to take the girls and move to Boston, where her family was. There was a job lined up for her, and her parents could help take care of the kids. I was so depressed I couldn't even fight her on it. I didn't know what to do. I didn't have the tools to help or fix anything.

Without my family and without a job, there was no reason to keep our home, so I put it on the market. I couldn't bear walking through the silent house and seeing the empty bedrooms. I stopped sleeping in my bed and lay on the couch. I let myself and the house go.

As a result, the house wasn't in any shape to sell—or even be viewed. I stopped caring and was ready to let it go back to the bank. I'd gotten a small severance package when my job ended, but money was running out quickly. I applied for unemployment, but the amount I was going to receive made me shudder.

I sent what money I could to Julie and the kids, and she was reasonable about it. Julie's parents stepped in and took over the mortgage as an investment for Julie and the kids. Our children had grown up in that house, and Julie wasn't ready to let it go. The stipulation was I needed to move out, which I did, into a small one-bedroom apartment.

Weeks turned into a month, and while I was working small temp jobs, I wasn't making nearly what I had at Nu-Horizon. I put in applications daily, but there were no bites.

This was about the time the cough developed. Even when it worsened, I ignored it. I wasn't a smoker, so it couldn't possibly be anything serious. I laid off the booze and began eating healthier. I felt this was a sign that I was getting back in control of my life. But sometimes, we wait too long to make changes.

In addition to neglecting my family, I had also failed to take care of my health. I hadn't been to a doctor in years. Finally the cough got bad enough that I couldn't ignore it. One night I was coughing so much I had blood in my mouth. Not long after noticing that, I blacked out.

I woke up in an ER and couldn't remember how I got there. Later Julie said I called and then dropped the phone. I had no recollection of any of it. She called 911, and the fire department had to break through my door. I was embarrassed to learn I was passed out on the floor, half-dressed, and I had to be taken out that way for all my neighbors to see. My mother would have been proud because at least I was wearing clean underwear.

The doctors had grave news. Not only did I have masses in my lungs, but there were masses elsewhere in my body. In fact, they believed cancer had developed in my colon and had spread. A simple colonoscopy could have caught it sooner and saved my life.

A week later, I began treatment, but the prognosis was not good: stage 4 cancer. My oncologist gave me three months to live. That was six months ago.

I stopped chemo a few weeks ago because it just makes me too sick, and what's the use? I'm going to die anyway, and it would only extend my life a little longer. I lost my apartment a couple of weeks ago because I couldn't keep up with the rent or bills. I barely have enough energy to get out of bed, let alone do temp jobs loading trucks at the meatpacking plant.

I stay at the homeless shelter down the street, but I have to leave during the day. I was going to the soup kitchen for food, but I've been getting weaker and weaker. The soup kitchen is too far to go, so I started asking for food at the train station. Some people give me money, and others give me leftovers if they have it.

My self-esteem is in the toilet, and I'm just counting the days until I die. I still have a life insurance policy that's paid off, so at least I'll be leaving something for my family. I'm worth more dead than alive.

Chapter 4:

RUNNING OUT OF TIME

Alex sat speechless for a few moments to fully absorb what had happened to his friend. It was all too shocking and terrible to contemplate. He looked at Teddy's sandwich, and there was still just one bite taken out of it. His coffee sat mostly untouched too.

"Why didn't you reach out to your parents? You don't have to be homeless. I'm sure they would have helped you."

"I tried to talk to my dad after I was let go from Nu-Horizon," Teddy replied. "He and I haven't been close for some time. He's been critical of most of my life decisions. But I swallowed my ego and called him. He laughed and told me if I had listened to him, I wouldn't be in the position I was in. He told me I was a man and that I needed to work out my financial and family issues on my own and not come home crying about my problems. Mom tried to reach out to me on her own, but I never returned her calls. I felt Dad was right. I needed to figure things out on my own. "

"Did you tell them you're sick?"

"No. Even cancer is something I need to take care of on my own. If I'm being really honest, I haven't wanted my father's pity or his lectures. It all seems stupid now—really stupid. I'm dying now, and I can't bring myself to call them."

"Why didn't you reach out to your friends? To me?"

"Since getting the diagnosis, I've taken a real hard look at myself. Because of my misplaced pride and brittle male ego, I've tried to stand like a lone wolf, and in doing so, I've pushed my family and friends out of my life."

"But I—"

"Let me finish, Alex. Like my health, I've waited too long to make amends. I feel like I don't deserve anyone's empathy or support. I don't want to burden anyone with my issues— especially people I care about. And . . . I'm embarrassed by my life and how I look." Teddy looked as though he was about to cry.

"That's crazy, man," said Alex. "You know we would be there for you." But as the words came out of his mouth, he reflected on how he too, had neglected to stay in contact with his friends. A knot formed in his stomach. Could he become like Teddy? Was it too late for him too?

"I know," replied Teddy. "But I just couldn't do it after all this time."

"Surely Julie could help you now that you're homeless and ill."

Teddy looked at his sandwich for a minute and took a raspy breath. "No one knows where I am right now or that I have cancer."

"What?" Alex was shocked. "Are you kidding? I thought you said she called 911 when you passed out."

"Yeah, but I told her I was fine. Just a little dehydrated." Teddy's eyes remained on the uneaten sandwich, and a tear rolled down his nose. "I didn't tell anyone. I have not talked to Julie or the kids in about two months, and my parents even longer. I don't have a phone anymore, so they can't reach me. I . . . I just don't want anyone's pity. You know?"

Alex let the silence sit. His heart was broken, and so many thoughts about what to do floated through his head. He couldn't just shake hands and walk out of the coffee shop and wish him the best of luck. He had to do something.

He thought about that a moment more and looked at his friend, who was dying. The problem was Alex didn't have the luxury of time. With everything happening at work, he couldn't just take off and help his friend. Teddy needed help, and Alex might be the last person that could help him.

"Seeing you today . . . I . . ." Teddy took another raspy breath and looked up at Alex. "I didn't realize it until we sat down here, but . . . Alex, I don't want to die alone."

Alex's throat clamped, and he was having difficulty catching his breath. Was Teddy really dying? How could this be? In college, he was a health nut and worked out all the time. He made fun of Alex's diet, which mainly consisted of ramen and pizza, while he drank protein shakes and ate lean meats and raw vegetables. The man who stood before Alex was a diminished version of the guy who could run ten miles and bench-press three hundred pounds. It was too surreal to contemplate.

As unreal as it seemed, Alex's friend had just proclaimed he didn't want to die alone, yet he was alone. He was alienated from his family and was living on the street. Alex felt morally obligated to do something about it.

"The first thing we need to do is get you to a doctor," he said.

"No. No more doctors. There's nothing more they can do for me."

"Are you sure?"

"Yes, I'm sure," Teddy replied with some irritation.

"Well, then we need to get you off the streets. I could give you some money. You could buy some food and get a hotel room for a few nights."

Teddy's sunken eyes grew wide. "No way. I couldn't impose Alex. Besides, what would happen after a few days? The shelter is fine. They have a bed reserved for me. I'll be fine."

Alex was uncomfortable. He wanted to help Teddy, but if Teddy was too proud to accept his help, then what?

Teddy began standing up, and without thinking, Alex placed a hand on his arm and gently sat him back down.

"I don't know what to say Teddy. How can I help?"

"You've done enough, Alex. Really. I can take this sandwich with me. I can go down into the station and stay warm until the shelter opens back up."

Alex reached into his wallet and offered him what he had. "Come on Teddy, I need to help you somehow. I wouldn't feel right if I just let you go back out there in the freezing cold. Let me call you a taxi, and I'll book a room for you."

"Alex, it's fine." Teddy only took one of the twenties. "If it makes you feel better, I'll take this. It will feed me for a few days. Listen, I have been surviving just fine."

The two sat in silence. Then Teddy got his mostly uneaten sandwich wrapped up to go.

"It was really good seeing you again, Alex. I appreciate the food and money." With that, he walked out without saying another word.

Harriet placed a coffee to go on the table. "I know it's none of my business, and you can tell me to butt out, but I just heard what your friend had to say."

"And?"

"And you are just going to let him leave like that? The man is dying, and you think a twenty is going to solve his problems. The only thing it solved was that it made *you* feel better."

Alex was about to argue with her but stopped. "You're right," he admitted. "But what else was I supposed to do?"

"Do you have room at your house?"

"Are you crazy?" Alex asked a little too loudly. A couple of heads turned. "Are you crazy?" he said quieter.

"Is it crazy? Or is it the right thing to do?"

"My wife would never let be bring home a homeless man."

"How do you know? Have you asked her? Do you not believe your wife would be charitable enough to help one of your friends who was dying? Who did you marry?"

Again, Alex couldn't argue with her. He was the one who was uncomfortable. Sure, he'd love to help a friend, but he just didn't have the bandwidth to have him stay. He had such a tight schedule, and there were the kids to consider. What would they think of a sick man living in their house?

"Sheri, of course, would take him in. I can't even drive past a stray cat on the street without her asking me to turn around and pick it up. That's why we have three cats living at our house now." Alex was about to say more but caught himself. Was he saying that stray cats were more welcome than his dying friend? "OK. OK, I hear what you're saying."

Harriet smiled. "I'm not saying anything."

"You sure you're just a coffee shop owner and not some sort of mentalist getting into my head?"

"I didn't intend to get into your head," said Harriet as she wiped down the table. "I merely asked you some questions. You filled in the rest."

She was right. It still felt like some kind of Jedi mind trick.

· · · · · ·

Alex looked for Teddy before he went to the office, but Teddy was nowhere to be seen. Alex was distracted all day at work, thinking about what he should do. Harriet had acted as a mirror to his actions, and what Alex saw was not pretty. He just didn't know how else to handle the situation. Obviously, handing Teddy money was the solution.

Alex left twenty minutes before five, which was totally out of character for him. He wanted to beat the rush to see if he could find Teddy and apologize for his insensitivity, even though he still had no idea what else he could do to help his old friend.

EVERYONE IS AFRAID

Alex looked, but Teddy was nowhere to be seen. He looked around inside the station, and still no Teddy. Alex hoped he hadn't really screwed up.

He boarded the train and remembered something from the *WealthyWellthy* podcast. Someone talking about shields and vulnerability being a source of strength. Did Teddy have shields, and were they killing him? Alex remembered something else from the podcast—something about *The Story in Your Head* podcast. With a quick search, he found the "Shields" episode to distract him on the ride home.

EVERYONE IS AFRAID

Chapter 5:

AFTER-DINNER TALK

Alex didn't want to bring up the topic of Teddy at dinner. He wanted to talk to Sheri alone, so he offered to do the dishes.

"OK . . ." Sheri looked at her husband suspiciously. "Spill it!"

Steve and Lucy ran to their rooms, and Alex hauled the dishes to the kitchen and started washing up.

"I don't know what you mean?"

"One: you're home early from work. And two: now you've volunteered to help with the dishes. What's going on? Is everything OK at work?" Sheri asked.

The reality was Alex got home at the time he was supposed to, but he was chronically working late hours.

"Yeah, everything is fine at work," he said. "I ran into an old friend from college today."

"Oh? Who?"

"Teddy. You remember me talking about him?"

"He was part of that crazy Breakfast Club kind of group you ran with, right? He was the most likely to succeed, I think you told me."

"Yeah, that's Teddy. And yeah, he succeeded, just as I thought he would."

Alex was stalling because he didn't know how to say what he wanted to.

"So, where did you see him?" Sheri asked.

"Oh . . . I bumped into him at the train station." That was a bit of an understatement. "We had breakfast this morning."

"On a workday? You? Breakfast?" Sheri pressed the back of her hand against Alex's forehead. "You don't feel like you have a fever." She giggled.

"Yeah, we had coffee and food at Harriet's."

Alex needed to get to the point, but he was having difficulty. What was he dreading?

"So, how is he doing these days?"

That was it. That was the question he was dreading.

"Well, he lost his job and has had a hard time finding work."

"Did you offer to help him find a job? You have a lot of connections around Chicago through your firm." Sheri began drying some of the pots and pans with a towel.

"Yeah, but . . . he can't work right now."

"How come?"

Here it comes. This is the moment.

"He's sick. He has stage 4 cancer."

Sheri stopped drying and looked at Alex. "He has what?"

"He neglected seeing a doctor and getting a checkup, and it caught up with him. He has colon cancer that has spread through his body."

"Oh my. That's awful. Is he getting treatment? Can he get better?"

"They gave him a few months to live, and he survived past that date. But he stopped treatments. He looked terrible. I don't believe he has long."

"Does he have a wife and kids? This must be terrible for them."

"Yes, he has a wife and two little girls, but they don't know," Alex said.

"How can that be?"

"He was having marital problems about the time he lost his job. His wife took possession of their home because he couldn't afford it."

"Where is he living now?"

That was the second question Alex had been dreading.

"He's at a homeless shelter."

"He's what?"

"He doesn't have any money or any other place to stay. He's estranged from his parents, and because he worked so much, he doesn't have any friends to call on."

"He could have called you," Sheri said.

"That's what I told him."

"So, is he at the shelter now?"

"I guess so."

"Alex, you didn't leave your dying friend penniless without a place to stay, did you?"

A lump formed in Alex's throat. "It sounds much worse when you say that. I offered him some money to get a room and some food, but he would only take a twenty."

"And?"

"And what? That's it. I felt bad about it, and I tried to look for him to give him more money. But I couldn't find him at the station."

Sheri put down her dish towel and walked out of the room.

Alex followed her down the hall, and she opened the closet and slipped on her heavy coat.

"Where are you going?" Alex asked.

"You mean where are *we* going? I'll call next door to see if Betty can watch the kids, and then *we* will go to every homeless shelter until we find your friend. And then he is coming back home with us."

Alex grabbed his keys off the hook and put on his coat. He felt ashamed that he hadn't called home to Sheri when he was talking with Teddy. He trotted to the car and turned it on so it could heat up, and soon Sheri was in the passenger's seat.

"Betty is coming over, and I told the kids we'd be home soon with a house guest."

"I'm sorry, Sheri, I just . . . I'm so busy, and I didn't want to burden you. How long is he going to stay?"

"It isn't a burden to help another human being, Alex. We're both busy but not busy enough to turn away from a dying man when we have the room to take him in. We'll figure this out, but in the meantime, he deserves a real bed and real food."

Alex shifted the car into drive. "I'm pretty sure I know the shelter he's staying at. It's near the station. Again, I'm sorry."

Sheri put her hand on Alex's shoulder and said, "Alex, I'm not the one you need to apologize to. Besides, you're doing something to correct the situation, and that's what really matters."

Parking wasn't too bad downtown that time of night, but the wind sweeping off Lake Michigan was brutal. It cut right through the warmest of coats. Alex couldn't imagine what Teddy must be experiencing living on the streets. Teddy had a place to sleep at night, but during the day he was panhandling, and it wasn't much warmer then.

On the ride over, Sheri and Alex barely talked. Alex didn't know if she was mad at him or upset at the news of a dying man in a homeless shelter. It didn't matter because it was Alex's fault, and he felt the burden of it. Sheri was right. They had a guest room that had hardly been used. Their fridge and pantry were always full, and Sheri was an excellent cook. Alex kicked himself for not trusting that his wife would have been fine with Teddy staying. Alex didn't even need to ask—he just told her the story, and Sheri jumped into action. He recalled his earlier conversation with Harriet and had to admit that he'd been using Sheri as an excuse. He'd been so busy lately that he couldn't imagine taking on the responsibility of caring for a sick friend. Instead of opening his wallet, Alex reflected that he should have opened his heart a bit more. He hoped Teddy would give him a second chance to make this right.

. . . . . .

They did find Teddy, and he looked very surprised to see them.

After Sheri and Teddy had exchanged pleasantries, Alex got right to the point. "Listen, Teddy, I want to apologize for earlier. I was busy and wasn't thinking straight. I should have offered you some more help. I—"

"Don't worry, Alex," said Teddy. "I don't expect anything from you. I haven't seen you in years. We're more strangers than close acquaintances. I was just happy to spend some time with you."

This wasn't going to be easy. Even if Alex offered a place, he doubted Teddy would take it. The old Teddy would have been too proud for that.

"I understand that this might be awkward," said Sheri. "You barely know me, but I've heard about you and your antics for years. I don't feel like you're a stranger. I feel like you're a friend I just hadn't met yet."

This put a smile on Teddy's face. Leave it to Sheri. She always knew the right things to say.

"So, as our friend, I would like to invite you to stay at our house," Sheri said.

"Well . . . I . . . It would be too much."

Sheri crossed her arms. "I'm not taking no for an answer, Teddy. I can't bear to think of you being homeless and without family or friends to support you. You don't want to see me cry, do you?" Her eyes welled up.

"No, no, of course not. I don't know if Alex told you that I'm sick."

"Yes, and it's all more the reason to stay with people who will look after you."

"You have to say yes, Teddy. I guarantee you, I'll sleep here tonight if you don't," Alex said.

"OK," Teddy conceded. "Just for a little bit, though. At least until it warms up a bit."

"Teddy, you will stay as long as you need to and not a second less," Sheri said. "I don't care if I have to adopt you as my son. You are going to have a home to stay in."

Now it was Teddy's turn to hold back tears. "I don't know what to say. I've really screwed up my life royally. I never expected anyone to . . . to care anymore. You have no idea how this makes me feel."

"Can you tell me as you're packing your things and heading out the door?" Sheri held her hand close to her mouth and whispered, "There are people staring, and we just have one spare room. We can't take everyone!"

That made both Teddy and Alex laugh.

On the ride home, Alex reflected on what had transpired. Once Teddy had agreed to stay at the house, all of Alex's worries from the past few weeks began melting away, and a weight that was on his shoulders—one he hadn't realized was there—lifted. Had he been such a fool that he hadn't seen what was truly important in life? If he was in a spot like Teddy, would he find himself alone and hopeless? Was he the one who had his shields up and couldn't be vulnerable?

Alex had been so busy the past few years trying to impress everyone at work that he'd been neglecting Sheri and the kids. So many times, he'd made promises: once he got the next big case and the next big check, he would have more time to spend with them. Alex's family supported him, but he could see the disappointment in their eyes. He didn't know how to relax anymore. Even when he had time off, he either worried about his job or would find himself magically teleporting to his office to work on a project.

His thoughts spiraled. How many milestones had he missed with Lucy and Steve? Lucy's dance recitals. Steve's T-ball games. Kindergarten graduations. The school holiday parties. Alex was even late to Lucy's birthday party because a client needed to vent, and he took the call even though it was on a Saturday.

It was time to get his life straight, and the first thing he needed to do was help his friend Teddy.

Chapter 6:

STAY OR GO

The next morning everyone was around the table at breakfast. Teddy had cleaned up a bit and was wearing Alex's pajamas, but they hung like drapes on his emaciated frame. Teddy had insisted he had only a few months to live. From his appearance, Alex thought it might be less. Surely, modern medicine could do better. Teddy had been so full of life. How could he have been drained of vitality like this? Maybe he just needed a second opinion.

The kids loved the idea of having a house guest and asked a million questions at breakfast. Mostly they wanted to hear embarrassing stories about Alex as a reckless college student. Alex appreciated that Teddy edited the R-rated tales into G-rated versions.

Sheri rushed the kids off to school and then returned. Alex looked at his watch. He was going to be late to work.

"Thanks for all this," began Teddy. "I won't stay long."

"Nonsense," said Sheri. "As I said, you will stay as long as you need to."

"Have you considered going back for treatment? Maybe get a second opinion?" Alex asked.

"I've received enough opinions, and the chemo was worse than cancer. I'd only be prolonging the inevitable."

"That doesn't sound like the Teddy I know," said Alex. "The Teddy I know wouldn't back away from any fight."

Teddy squirmed in his seat a little.

"That Teddy is long gone, Alex. I'm no longer the guy you knew in college. Besides, I've made my decision."

Sheri frowned at Alex as a warning.

"But what about your kids?" Alex pressed. "Don't you want to spend time with them? Don't they deserve as much time as possible?"

Teddy was clearly getting irritated now. "Alex, I appreciate you're trying to help. I haven't seen my kids in months, and frankly, that's a good thing. You think I want them to remember me this way?" He held up his skeletal arms, resembling a scarecrow.

"I suppose not," Alex replied.

"Alex, I'm sick and dying. I want my kids to remember me when I was successful and healthy. Not some derelict on the street."

Sheri stepped in. "That's enough, Alex. Teddy has the right to make his own decisions."

Alex bowed his head a bit. He kept making bad assumptions, but there was so little time. He couldn't just sit back and watch his friend die and not try something. Was not wanting to let Teddy die one of his shields?

"While you look great in my husband's PJs, I think you need some better clothes of your own," Sheri continued.

"No, I couldn't . . ." Teddy began.

"Teddy, dear, it would hurt my feelings if you refused my offer to shop for you."

"How can I refuse?"

"You can't!" Alex chuckled. His phone beeped with a message from his assistant: *Where are you? People are asking about you. What should I tell them?*

Alex hesitated before sending a reply. What was he going to tell everyone? He was working on the biggest deal of his career, which required him to be at work all day, but he had just committed to helping his friend. This was insanity. He couldn't just abandon work.

Alex's gut twisted as he thought about his client and his friend. There was no easy solution. The only thing stopping Alex from helping Teddy was Alex himself. He was the one who controlled his insane schedule. Had he been using that schedule as a shield to avoid being vulnerable with Sheri?

Alex reminded himself that he wasn't alone on the project. Last year the firm had hired Todd. He was young, energetic, and ambitious. He had offered to help in any way he could. He knew the client and the deal just as well as Alex did, yet Alex had shut him down or taken away responsibilities whenever it seemed like Todd was becoming more involved than *he* was. But Jim Conner—the older brother in the firm and Alex's boss—had insisted that Todd be a part of the deal and attend the client meetings and negotiations. It made Alex extremely nervous; he was sure Todd would take over the account. Alex's greatest fear was that Todd would become a partner before he did.

If Alex asked Todd to take over for a while, he feared he could be signing his doom. Todd could swoop in and take over, and Alex would be pushed out. He pondered whether he should put in his application for flipping burgers down the street.

"I'll help you with the dishes, Sheri. I'll be right back, Teddy."

Sheri and Alex entered the kitchen and began rinsing and loading the dishes into the dishwasher.

"Helping me with dishes two times in a row? I need to call the local news station!" commented Sheri.

"I have a dilemma. I'm not sure what I should do. I've been out of the office all morning, and they're asking where I am. I don't want to leave you to take care of Teddy by yourself. Maybe I could call someone from social services? If I'm not at work, I'm not sure about the deal."

"Will the deal fail if you aren't there?" Sheri's voice was neutral.

Alex had to think about that. In addition to Todd and Jim, there was an army of clerks and assistants working on it. Alex was the face of the deal, but a lot of the other work was being done by the rest of the team.

"If I don't show up, then someone else will have to give the presentation," Alex replied.

"Will you lose the account if someone else does the presentation?"

"No, we'll get the account. The presentation is merely to seal the deal."

"Is someone else capable of handling the preparation and presentation?"

"Todd could do it, sure," Alex admitted. "But then he could take all the credit."

"You've told me before that you like Todd. Has he given you any indication he would take all the credit and leave you out of it? You've worked hard to hook this client. Everyone knows that."

"I guess. I'm just worried. He's a hotshot and does great work. I have a lot riding on this, Sheri." The more Alex heard himself, the less he liked what he was saying.

"Did Jim promise you partnership because of this deal?"

"No, not exactly. But this contract will make them millions over the next few years."

"You've brought them other clients, Alex, which have made them a lot of money. How is this one different?"

That was a great question. No one had promised Alex anything related to the deal. He assumed an account this large would be a sure way into a partner seat, but it wasn't a guarantee. He had been working long hours for years and had brought them many clients and tons of billable hours. He had talked to Jim about a partnership, and Jim had said he was in line for it, but Alex had failed to ask for any more details. He didn't want to rock the boat and ask too many questions. Perhaps he should take a more direct approach than guessing.

"It's really simple, Alex. Either stay home and help your friend or win a new client that may or may not lock in a partnership. The real question is, is this client worth it? Also, why would you assume I couldn't handle things for you while you're working? I've taken care of two kids every day since they were born. Helping out an adult will be a piece of cake."

Sheri had a very practical way of distilling complicated situations into simple parts. Alex felt a little ashamed that, once again, he hadn't trusted his wife.

"Of course I think you can handle it," he responded. "But I feel like I'm just abandoning him again like I did the other day. On the other hand, I thought you wanted me to get ahead and become a partner. If I let this deal go, I could be passing up my one chance to find a permanent seat at the firm. Is that what we want? What I have been working so hard for?"

Sheri sighed. "That is *your* dream, Alex, not ours. Lucy, Steve, and I have everything we need except more time with you. All I can do is say what I would do. It's your choice."

Sheri's questions were forcing Alex to really look at what he cared about, what was important to him. Sheri, Lucy, Steve—and now Teddy. Teddy needed help, and Alex would choose to be there for him.

"Thank you, honey. I love you," he said as he kissed his wife's forehead.

"I love you too."

Chapter 7:

TIME OFF

Before Alex could consider taking off for a few days, he needed to talk to his boss.

"Is Jim available for a few minutes, Sally?" Alex asked. He was standing in front of Jim Conner's office. It was tastefully decorated in dark woods and polished brass. Alex had considered calling in first but decided that he needed to talk to Jim directly.

Alex was nervous, as this was unlike anything he had ever done. His gut was telling him to bolt out of the office and get back to his desk to work on the presentation. His heart was committed to helping Teddy. He couldn't live with the consequences of abandoning him—it was clear there was no one else looking out for him. Sheri would do a great job looking after Teddy, but it wasn't fair to leave her with the total burden of it. Besides, there was a reason he ran into Teddy that day at the station. It was life trying to tell Alex something, and he was committed to figuring it out.

Sally hung up the phone and said, "He'll be with you in a moment."

Alex sat down on one of the plush leather chairs. This was the kind of office his father had dreamed of for him. This was what he was working so hard to have. He had spent many nights arguing with Sheri about working long hours, explaining that he needed to put in that time if he wanted to be successful. Once he was made partner, he could provide a more secure future for her, Steve, and Lucy. She always said she understood, but her face betrayed that she did not agree with everything Alex said.

Sheri wanted him to connect more with her and the kids. Alex wanted to do that too. He just needed to anchor his career a bit more, and then he could have some breathing room. To make up for his absence, Alex bought Sheri expensive gifts. She always thanked him but never seemed overly excited about the gifts. Alex would accuse her of being ungrateful, and sometimes he had to sleep in the guest bedroom to prevent any further arguing. He tried to convince himself he was giving her time to cool off, but in truth, it was Alex who was irritated and showing his anger. He blamed Sheri for not seeing everything he was doing for her and the kids.

Alex thought it was her fault. What if it wasn't?

Before Alex could ponder the question further, the door opened, and Jim Conner came out with his great big smile. He was like a second father to Alex and had taken him under his wing. Jim was eternally optimistic and generous. His great passions were the Cubs and his grandkids. He couldn't stop talking about either whenever he and Alex met for drinks or saw each other at a company party. He seemed to be happy with his life and with what he had accomplished. Jim was Alex's role model, and Alex hoped one day to be as successful and as loved as Jim was.

Jim extended his hand, and when Alex gripped it, Jim patted his arm. He looked Alex directly in the eyes and said, "It is so great to see you. Come on in."

This was the usual way Jim greeted everyone. People would comment that they felt valued and "seen" by Jim. They trusted him implicitly and valued any time they could spend with him.

Instead of sitting behind his desk, Jim offered Alex a seat across from him. "Would you like something to drink?"

"No, I'm fine, thank you."

"So what can I do you for?"

Alex's mouth became dry. How could he ask for some time off at such a pivotal moment? He felt like a selfish ass for even contemplating it. Jim had been very generous whenever Alex had asked for help. Alex never felt it was an inconvenience to ask him to assist with a case or soothe a client's anger over the phone. So why should this be different?

The issue was that the firm was Jim's baby. He had built it with his brother and his best friend from college. They liked making money—a lot of money. What Alex was about to ask could jeopardize a huge account and profit margins.

Alex started to say something, but nothing came out. He cleared his throat and said, "On second thought, I could really use a glass of water."

"Not a problem," Jim said. He filled a tumbler with ice from a bucket on his bar. "Is everything OK at home? You look like something is weighing heavy on you."

"Sheri and the kids are fine. Yes, something is weighing heavy. It's . . . my friend. Teddy."

Alex accepted the glass Jim offered him and took a long drink. He paused to gather his thoughts and courage. "Please don't fire me," he thought.

"Oh? What's wrong with Teddy?"

"I haven't seen him in a long time. Since we graduated from college, actually. But I saw him at the train station, and we had coffee at Harriet's."

"She has the best coffee, doesn't she? And she always knows your order and has it ready."

"Yeah, Harriet is great. So my friend Teddy is sick. Like *dying* sick." Alex could feel a lump forming in his throat. As he said the words out loud, it became even more clear that his friend might die soon.

He felt helpless because he couldn't erase that truth and was at a loss for what he could do in the meantime. Alex knew he wanted to spend time with Teddy, but he hadn't a clue what Teddy might need. Maybe taking time off right now wasn't a good plan. He supposed the easiest solution was to ask Teddy what he needed rather than blindly guess what it might be.

"Oh, Alex, I am sorry to hear that," said Jim with real compassion in his voice.

"That's why I wanted to talk to you. He doesn't have anyone around him right now. He lost his job, he's separated from his

EVERYONE IS AFRAID

wife and kids, and he's estranged from the rest of his family and friends. He's refusing to reach out to them. He's all alone, and I really feel like he needs my help. He has terminal cancer, and he said to me . . . He said he doesn't want to die alone."

Jim stood up and walked to the bar. He poured some whiskey into a glass and dropped in a large ice cube. The clock on the wall said it was noon. This was odd for Jim.

He stood in front of the large window that overlooked the city and swirled his glass. The longer he stood, the more nervous Alex became. What was he going to say? Alex was sure he was going to say he was off the project permanently. Or maybe that if he took time off, he might as well not come back at all. It was an irrational disaster fantasy, but nonetheless, the thought gripped Alex. Attorney competition was high, especially in a well-established firm like Conner, Conner, and Moore. It was like Alex was running in for the touchdown and had fumbled on the one-yard line.

Jim remained silent for so long that Alex thought perhaps he was supposed to leave. Jim was done with him, so Alex needed to take a hint. Alex put his glass on a coaster and cleared his throat.

"I'm sorry," said Jim. "What you said made me think about my friend Roger. He passed away last year." He took a deep drink of his whiskey and turned to Alex. "Remember when I took a week off last November? That was so I could go to his funeral. Only Sally knew why I was gone. Everyone else thought I'd gone to Aspen to ski. Technically I did go to Colorado, but it sure wasn't for skiing."

Alex didn't know how to respond. Jim was sharing something very personal and obviously emotional, and Alex didn't want to interrupt him, so he nodded silently.

"Roger had children later in life, and so he had a son just graduating from high school. The sadness on that kid's face still haunts me. Do you want to know the worst part, Alex?"

"Yes."

"I hadn't seen Roger in a couple of years. We were always too busy to connect."

Alex could see tears welling up in his boss's eyes. He felt like he should say or do something, but he didn't know what. The feeling of being lost and hopeless seemed to be as intense for Jim as it was for Alex.

"I didn't even know he was sick, Alex. If he had told me, I would have gone to him immediately. Do you know how many times I canceled our plans for dinner or a drink when he was in town? How many times I could have said yes and made some room in my schedule to visit him? Or for him to come here with his family? Too many. I just never made time, thinking I had all the time in the world left. It turns out he didn't. Now I . . . I didn't have a chance to say goodbye to a good friend."

Listening to Jim Conner tell his story solidified Alex's resolve. He needed to be there for Teddy and needed to stop worrying about things that mattered less. Alex had to trust things would work out at the firm because he had limited time to help Teddy.

"I know you didn't come here to listen to me blubbering over my regret, Alex. How can I help you?"

"I think I need to take some time off," Alex said, shocked the words were coming out so easily. "I know this isn't a good time, but Todd can take over the presentation Friday. He's up to speed and has been working as hard as I have to be sure we're able to close this deal."

There it was. It was all out. Alex felt like he'd just given away his best chance to become a partner. He hoped he could live with the decision, no matter the outcome.

"How much time do you think you'll need?" Jim asked.

Alex couldn't read him. Was he irritated? Supportive? "Maybe a week? To be sure he has what he needs and is comfortable. To be honest, I'm not sure what he'll need. I'll get back to the office as soon as I can. After that, I can visit him during lunch breaks and after work."

"Wait—you take lunch breaks?" Jim had a slight grin on his face.

"Well, I uh . . ."

"Alex, it's OK. I'm kidding with you! Well, sort of. You never leave this office. You're here before I arrive, and you're still here when I leave. I worry about you."

"You do?"

"Yes! Of course! You're working all the time. When do you take time off to spend with your family? Have you ever taken a vacation or even holiday leave?"

He was right. Alex didn't take time off because he thought the firm wanted to see how dedicated he was. This was Alex's way of trying to get ahead and get noticed. It was the way his father had succeeded, so it made sense to Alex. Could he have been wrong?

"The partners and I want everyone who works for us to have a balanced life," Jim continued. "We know how hard this work is, and we have seen too many promising attorneys burn out. We don't need more of that."

"So, would you be OK with me taking some time off this week? I feel guilty leaving this all to Todd and you. I could come back for a couple of hours Friday if you need me to help prep."

"I wouldn't hear of it, Alex. Yes, the timing is not ideal, but we don't get to choose the timing life has for us. It sounds like your friend needs you right now, and that trumps everything else. Don't be like me and regret *not* taking that time. Hard work is important, but it's not worth sacrificing everything else in your life."

"I guess you're right," Alex said. This conversation was not going the way he'd expected. Maybe he'd been approaching the partner thing all wrong. If they were looking for partners who had a work-life balance, then Alex wasn't their guy. He had a lot of thinking to do. "I have to confess, I was a bit nervous coming in to talk to you about this. We had mentioned the possibility of me becoming a partner some time back, and I've taken that to heart. I was worried that taking time off right in the middle of this deal would . . . hurt my chances."

Jim's eyes widened. "Of course we value the deals we make and the clients we acquire. That's what keeps the lights on. But we value people most of all. Our people. We want partners who understand our vision. Being a martyr is not part of that vision. Taking time off for family and people who matter to you isn't a sign you aren't partner material. Quite the contrary."

"You don't know what a relief that is to hear."

"I want you to call me if you need anything—anytime, day or night. I am here to support you, Alex. This can be a trying and emotional time, and I want you to know that you are not alone. I'll have Todd call you if we can't figure out something here. I'll let you know how the presentation goes. I'm sure it will be brilliant, and the contract is pretty much in the bag. We couldn't have done it without you. When you come back, let's talk about your future, OK?"

Alex took a deep, calming breath. The worst was over, and it had turned out better than he could have imagined. Jim had said Alex wasn't alone. That was exactly what Teddy wanted. It kept bouncing around in Alex's head. If he hadn't been vulnerable with Jim, Jim would not have been vulnerable with him. This was so different from what Alex had imagined.

"I can't thank you enough," he said as he shook Jim's hand.

As stressful and uncomfortable as it had been to approach Jim with his dilemma, Alex's next task was going to be even more challenging. It was time to make some phone calls he wasn't looking forward to. He needed to call his friends from college and tell them what was going on. Alex could use the support of the old crew. That meant he needed to reach out to people he hadn't talked to in a long time. He hoped those conversations would go as smoothly as his meeting with Jim had.

EVERYONE IS AFRAID

Chapter 8:

BHAVANI—ER DOCTOR

The alarm blared. It was 5:30 a.m. To Bhavani, it seemed like mornings were happening earlier and earlier. Last night's double shift was rough. Five victims from a car crash because of a drunk driver. The driver had nothing but a broken ulna, but the family he hit was not so lucky. The father was in a coma with serious brain swelling. The mother's pelvis was broken, along with multiple ribs and her collarbone, and her hand was crushed. The attending surgeon wasn't sure he could save it. And the twins. Two little boys. Bhavani didn't even want to think about what had happened to them.

The car wreck victims had arrived half an hour before Bhavani was supposed to leave, so that's why she did a double. She wanted to be sure everyone was stable before she left. By the time she got home, she had just enough energy for a glass of wine, and she was asleep by the time her head hit the pillow. She wondered what time that was.

Bhavani got out of bed and almost screamed in the darkness. It was late morning, but the sun-blocking shades had been mercifully closed by her husband. Even though Bhavani couldn't see it, she knew what the sharp object was. Nelly had been in the room while she was at work, playing with her building blocks again.

The floor was a sharp plastic minefield, so Bhavani shone her phone's flashlight on the floor to make her way to the kitchen for some coffee. She had no idea how she had made it to bed unscathed but she figured she'd been so tired that even if she had stepped on something, she wouldn't have felt it.

Once Bhavani reached the kitchen, a fireball of anger crawled up her throat. Last night she'd just grabbed a glass and poured some wine before heading to bed. She hadn't really paid attention to the kitchen until now.

Frank must have decided it was pizza night. The kids loved pizza night. The dried flour on the counter and the sprinkles of cheese on the floor were the first clues. The leftover pizza on the pan sitting on top of the stove was the next.

Bhavani looked at her watch. She would have just enough time to clean the kitchen and get out the door for her afternoon shift. No time for Pilates today. She didn't understand Frank. Why did he have to leave a mess and let the kids run wild? Bhavani knew she should have been home for dinner, but things happened. She had hoped her husband could be a little more responsible and clean up after himself. Bhavani's mother would have grounded her a week—no, a month—if she'd left a mess like this.

She spent the next hour cleaning and scouring the kitchen. She left a note on the counter for the kids letting them know she was thinking of them and was sorry she hadn't seen them. Bhavani thought about the mess still in the bedroom. She'd have to deal with it when she got home.

She was thankful it was an in-house training day. She wasn't sure she could handle another full shift. There was talk about some deadly virus making the rounds, so the staff were getting a refresher on universal precautions.

At the break, she saw a missed call from a number she didn't recognize. A Chicago area code? Who did she know in Chicago? She was about to dismiss it as a robocaller when she saw there was a message:

> Hey, Bhavani. It's Alex. Long time, right? Uh. I wanted to talk to you. It's about, um, Teddy. I recently connected with him, and, well, he's in pretty bad shape. Can you give me a call when you have a moment?

Bhavani's heart filled and then sank. Alex? Teddy? How long had it been? Years! They had been in German club together in college, which led to an unlikely circle of friends. They did everything together and shared everything. Back then, they were destined to be friends forever.

What happened?

For Bhavani, it was college, med school, residency,

internship, a husband, and two little girls. There was too much going on, and she hadn't considered her college friends in years.

She texted a quick reply: *Alex, it is so good to hear from you! It has been way too long. I'm sorry to hear about Teddy, and I'd like to talk to you more. I'll call you tonight.*

. . . . . .

Bhavani was exhausted and had to work hard to stay focused during the rest of the presentation. The description of the virus was terrifying. It had started in Asia, and now it was showing up in the United States. Working in the ER, she would be on the front line. Now she'd have to be extra careful and wear a special mask and gloves at all times. It was easy to be lax in the ER because everyone was so busy running from patient to patient. Something about this virus felt different, and she needed to be diligent.

Bhavani arrived home just after five, and her girls gave her big hugs. They began talking over one another, showing her their schoolwork.

"Nelly, that handwriting is getting better," Bhavani said. "Keep working at it."

"But Mommy, I thought this was good. Mrs. Simpson said it was great."

"Oh, honey, it is, but we can always do better, right?"

"I guess," said Nelly. She was looking at the floor. "Daddy said it was perfect."

Bhavani took a deep breath. "I'm sure Daddy loved it, pumpkin, but in life, we can't just stop when we do something good once. We have to keep practicing until it's perfect every time."

"OK," Nelly said. Even though she was only seven, Nelly was a charmer. She was so much like her dad. Always kidding around and looking for the next fun thing. It was hard to get her focused on schoolwork. Mrs. Simpson said that she was a delight to have in the classroom but that it was sometimes hard to get her on task because she liked entertaining the other students. Bhavani would have to talk to Frank again about encouraging her to try harder instead of just saying everything she did was perfect.

Aurora, the eleven-year-old, was more like her mother. She was practical, a hard worker, and motivated. She even made her bed in the morning. Aurora never had too much time for fun things, even though she lived in the home of the King of Fun—Frank. Bhavani did feel a little bad that Aurora didn't have many friends.

The family had a dinner of salad, pork chops, and asparagus. Delicious and nutritious.

"I like it better when Daddy cooks," said Nelly as she pushed her food around her plate.

"It's OK to have pizza some nights, just not every night," Bhavani responded. Her phone buzzed, but she had a no-phone rule at dinner, so it would have to wait.

"And girls, please don't leave the kitchen like it was last night," Bhavani said as she cleared the table.

"I told you," said Aurora. "I told you Mom would be mad."

"But Daddy said it was OK. He said he would do them in the morning," snapped Nelly.

Bhavani was sure he did, and she shot Frank a look. He shrugged. "Who wants to have ice cream?" he asked.

Both girls raised their hands.

"Let's go get some at Farrell's and let Mommy have some relaxing time."

Bhavani could feel her blood pressure rising. "On a school night?"

"It's fine, honey. They have a late start time tomorrow. I'll have them back and in bed before you know it."

Before Bhavani could respond, the three of them ran into the garage. She looked over at the dishes in the sink. "Not this time, mister," she said. "They'll be waiting for you right where you left them."

Her phone buzzed again. It was a text from Alex: *Are you going to call me tonight? I don't want to bother you. But it's important.*

· · · · · ·

"I am so sorry, Alex," Bhavani said. "It's been a crazy couple of days."

"It is so great to hear your voice, Bhavani. I can't believe how long it's been."

The two old friends exchanged a few more pleasantries and caught up about work and family.

"Wow," Alex said. "You *have* been quite busy."

"It sounds like you have as well."

Alex became silent. Those few seconds stretched into awkwardness. Bhavani didn't want to drag out the conversation too long because Frank and the kids would be home soon. She needed to get the girls to bed, and then she needed to talk with Frank about a few things that needed to change.

"So . . . I saw Teddy for the first time since school," said Alex slowly.

"Yeah, don't think I've seen him since school either. We were thick as thieves back in the day. But you know . . . life happens. So where did you meet him?"

There was another long pause. It was so long that Bhavani thought she might have lost the connection. "Alex?" she asked.

He cleared his throat a couple of times. "I was going to work the other day, and there he was, at the train station, asking for help. Basically money. He's homeless."

"Homeless? How could that be? I haven't talked to him in forever, but I saw an old acquaintance from college about a year or so ago. She said he had a family and was killing it where he worked. Now he's homeless? How did that happen?"

Bhavani heard the garage door open, so she moved into the den.

"Listen, Alex. I hate to do this, but I might have to cut this short. My family just got home, and I have to get everyone squared away."

"Of course. I'll be fast. Teddy lost his job, his home, and his family moved away. He's very ill. I'm helping him every way I can at the moment, but honestly, I don't think he has very long."

Nelly came into the room, and Bhavani held up a finger and pointed at the phone. Nelly threw her arms up and stomped back out.

"That sounds awful," Bhavani responded. "He is so lucky you're there."

"Yeah, that's the thing, Bhavani. His one wish is not to die alone. We were all such close friends, and I was calling everyone in our group to see if maybe you could come for a visit. He might not have long."

This took Bhavani by surprise. It was hard to concentrate on the conversation, and Nelly's television began blaring in the other room.

"Just a second." Bhavani pushed Mute on the phone. "Nelly, it's time to go to bed now. Turn off the TV." She unmuted. "I'm so sorry, Alex. I'm going to have to go. As far as coming up there, I just can't right now. I may have some time I can take in a couple of months. Perhaps I can make a small family vacay out of it. But right now, I just can't. But please let him know I'm thinking of him and that I'll say some prayers for him."

Again, the agonizing silence.

"I know this is a burden on you," Bhavani continued. "If you need me to send some money to help, I'd be glad to."

"No, that's OK. We have it covered," said Alex. His voice sounded distant now. "I'll call you if there are any changes."

"I'd like that. I'll let you know if we can make it there."

The two said their goodbyes, and something in Bhavani's stomach didn't feel right. She was in the business of helping people and saving lives. She hadn't been completely honest with Alex—not only could she take time off right now, but her boss was actually insisting she take it. The administrators were big on preventing burnout.

But with the new virus and everything else going on, she needed to be close to home. She couldn't be across the US if another doctor called out and there was a hole in the schedule. She needed to be ready to cover shifts. Even though she was resolved in her decision, she still didn't feel great about it.

EVERYONE IS AFRAID

Chapter 9:

DESIREE—CLEANING BUSINESS OWNER

Buzz . . . Buzz . . . Buzz . . .

"Are you going to get that?" Kate asked her business partner, Desiree.

"What's the use of getting out of the office to have a meeting with you if I'm on the phone. Let it go to voice mail."

Desiree was lying big time, but she didn't know whether it was to fool Kate or herself. Each *buzz* rolled like an electric shock through Desiree's nervous system. She wanted to answer because there could be a million things going wrong at work. They had already called four times this morning, and each time the phone buzzed, Desiree's hand moved toward it in a Pavlovian response. Resisting was possible, but doing it upset her gut.

"You sure you want to have a meeting here rather than at the office?" Kate asked.

The coffee shop was busy, and it was difficult to hear one another over the whooshing of the milk frother. But meeting in the office would have been a bad idea—too many ears.

"Yes," Desiree said as she sipped her latte. "This is sub rosa and important. In fact, I'm going to ask you to keep what I'm about to tell you to yourself."

Kate adjusted herself in her seat and frowned a bit. "Sure, I guess. What's sub rosa?"

"It means secret. In the old days it meant death if you shared. So, there is no *I guess*, Kate. This is too important," Desiree snapped. She didn't mean for it to come across so strongly, but she was stressed just having this conversation.

"OK, OK. I promise," said Kate, sitting up a little straighter. "What's going on?"

Kate had been with Desiree from the start, four years ago. They'd begun in the back of a dry cleaner shop, taking orders for offices to be cleaned. Back then, they had been a small enough operation that they did paperwork and calls during the day and split up to clean offices by night. As they grew, they hired more people. Last year their sales had almost doubled, as did the size of their staff.

They'd expanded further and moved into a nice office in a fancy strip mall. Desiree was able to buy herself some toys to park in her garage. But even so, she was working all the time. During the day, she had to manage the office, do the finances, hire staff, order supplies, and figure out everything else. Kate helped, but

Desiree still felt she needed to check her work. They'd recently received a complaint that some trash cans weren't emptied, so Desiree needed to follow up on the jobs every night to be sure they were done to the company standard.

That didn't leave much time for a social or romantic life. She even worked weekends to catch up and had not had a vacation in over two years. Kate constantly asked what else she could do, but Desiree preferred to do tasks herself to make sure they were done correctly.

"You know the last six months have been tough, right?" Desiree asked.

"Yeah, since Jiffy Kleen came to town. They've outbid us on some jobs, but we'll get them back. They may be cheaper, but you know the quality is not as good. We have to be patient."

"Well, that's why I wanted to meet with you," Desiree said, and she took another sip of the coffee. It would have been good if there was big dollop of courage in that latte. "We can't wait. We need to let some people go. I don't think we're going to make payroll this month."

Kate almost spit out her coffee. "What?"

"I paid the bills, and with the loss of three accounts this month, we're spending more cash than we're bringing in. In fact, I may have to start cleaning some of the offices myself again."

"What? How? How did this happen? Why didn't you say anything sooner?" asked Kate. Her brows were knitted with concern now.

"I thought I had it all under control. I was trying to make

the numbers work and keep everyone happy, but I just can't," Desiree admitted.

"Of course you can't," said Kate. "I've told you, you need someone who knows what they're doing handling the finances."

"Kate, I know what I'm doing," Desiree said. Her pride was hurt. "I have run two other businesses. This isn't my first rodeo."

"Yes, you ran two other businesses . . . into the ground, though."

"Hey, that's not fair."

"Fair? What does fair have to do with it, Desiree?" Kate said. "I have warned you. When we started growing, we needed to let some of the daily stuff go and let professionals that know way more about things than we do handle it. I even showed you what it would cost. We could afford it, but you didn't believe me."

"I refused because I don't trust anyone to handle our money," Desiree countered. She didn't like where the conversation was headed.

Buzz . . . Buzz . . . Buzz . . .

Desiree picked up her phone, pushed the button to send the caller to voice mail, and slammed the phone onto the table.

"Desiree, how bad is it?" asked Kate in a softer tone.

"Really bad." Desiree hung her head. "We have to cut our staff in half."

Kate's eyes widened. "In half?"

"And . . . there's worse news."

"There's worse news than what you just shared?"

"I'm going to have to sell my car to make payroll and taxes this month, but then next month, if things don't pick up . . ."

Buzz . . . Buzz . . . Buzz . . .

Desiree answered the phone without looking at who was calling. "What is it? Can't you handle things there just one morning without me?"

"Uh . . . Desiree . . . This is Alex. Is this a bad time?"

It was a voice Desiree knew in another life—one that she had not heard in many years.

"Alex? I'm so sorry. I thought it was someone else," Desiree fumbled.

"Yeah, no problem. I know it's been a long time . . ."

There was a long pause. Desiree wasn't sure if he wanted her to speak first or what.

"Well, as you can tell, I'm a little busy at the moment," Desiree interjected. "I'll be heading off to lunch in a bit. Can I call you then?"

"Please. You now have my number."

She looked down. "Yep, I've got it."

"Great. Talk soon," said Alex, and he hung up.

Desiree turned back to Kate, who was scrolling on her phone. "I'm sorry, that was an old friend."

Kate continued to scroll on her phone without answering.

"What are you looking at?" Desiree prompted.

Kate glanced up at Desiree. "Besides fighting my instinct to update my résumé, I am looking up a friend who is a business and financial coach who owes me a favor. I have a friend. Let's talk to him before we talk to the staff, OK?"

Desiree took a deep breath. Kate was the eternal optimist. She just didn't grasp what state the business was actually in.

But whose fault was that? Desiree hadn't been sharing what was happening with her partner because she knew she should take care of it without worrying Kate. Now their business was going downhill fast. Desiree owed it to her to listen to someone else and give it one last try. Perhaps she could save her car in the process.

"All right," Desiree agreed. "It has to be yesterday, though. Time is not on our side."

. . . . . .

Desiree sat down at her favorite diner with her usual pastrami on rye. She looked at it with no appetite at all. She pulled out her phone and redialed her old friend's number.

"Hey, Alex, I'm sorry about earlier. There's a lot going on at work right now."

"I totally understand," said Alex. "I won't take up too much of your time. I'm calling you about Teddy."

"Wow, I haven't heard from Teddy in a long time. How's he doing? Must be living large while us stiffs are working ourselves into an early grave."

"Well . . . not exactly."

Over the next twenty minutes, Alex explained his meeting with Teddy and his condition. Desiree felt time slow down in the diner. Teddy and Desiree had been hallmates their senior year. He'd had so many dreams and big plans and seemed set up for success. How could he be penniless *and* dying?

"I . . . I can't believe it," Desiree said in shock. "I could send a little money if that would help. My business is in a . . . transition stage, so it could be a couple of weeks."

EVERYONE IS AFRAID

"He doesn't need money, Desiree. He needs his friends right now. I spoke to his doctor this morning. His prognosis is grim."

"How grim?"

"He doesn't have long. Doctors are not great at giving exact expiration dates."

"So, he could last a bit, then?"

"It's not something I would count on," replied Alex.

"As I said, my business is in a transition period, which means I'll have even less time than I do now. Maybe I could come in a few weeks or so."

There was silence on the other end of the phone.

"I understand," Alex finally replied. "I'm in a similar situation at my job. I decided to take the time, as I might not have time later."

"Yeah, but you work for a law firm, right? You probably have PPO insurance and a full 401(k), right? I'm just a small business owner. I don't get breaks and vacations. I feel guilty for eating out and not being in the office right now. When I'm away, bad things always happen. I'm sorry. Please let Teddy know I'm thinking of him and will try to see him as soon as I can."

After Desiree hung up the phone, she felt terrible. She and Teddy had shared so many private feelings in college. How could they have grown so far apart? He'd been someone she could rely on if she needed help. How could things have changed so much? In college, they vowed they would one day rule the world. Now Teddy was broke and sick, and Desiree was about to lose her business. Again.

Maybe she should go see Teddy. There was little she could do right now with the business. She tried to think positively about Kate's plan, but she didn't see that it would make much of a difference. Going to Chicago for a few days could help Desiree sort her life out a bit.

Buzz . . . Buzz . . . Buzz . . .

"Yeah?"

"Hey, some guys from Miratomi Plaza are here to see you," said Kate. "They said they had an appointment."

"Damn it," Desiree spat. "I totally forgot about it."

"Why are they here? You didn't mention a meeting."

"I know, I know. They have a lot of offices, and I thought I could pitch them on a contract."

"Well, I can do that. They keep looking at their watches."

"No, no, just delay them, and if they need to leave, then I will reschedule."

"Desiree. I am fully capable of talking to them. This could be the break we need. Let me do it."

"I know you mean well, Kate. But just let me handle it. I will be there in fifteen minutes."

"But—"

"Fifteen minutes. Just keep them there." Desiree hung up the phone before Kate could answer. She needed to concentrate on her business. Distractions like Teddy would just have to wait.

Chapter 10:

EVI–VIDEO GAME PROGRAMMER

"Yeah, Mom, I get it," Evi said for the tenth time in a row. "I'm too old to be single. I need a man beside me. I hear you."

"Your sisters already have children, Evi," her mother said.

How many times had they had this same talk? How many times just this week? Evi's mom didn't get it, and Evi doubted a woman in her seventies would ever understand that not everyone was interested in settling down and having two and a half kids. That wasn't how Evi saw her life, but her mother had a clear vision of what Evi's duties were.

"You do like men, don't you? I mean, if you don't, that's fine," her mother continued. "This is a new century, and you could adopt. Or you could get that artificial *seminary* thing."

Evi smacked her head. "Are you about done bludgeoning me, Mom?" She really wanted the conversation to end.

"I'm just saying. I would love some more grandkids. I could help you in raising them. It would also give me a chance to see you more."

"Oh, Mom—it's another call. I have to take it," Evi lied.

"Well, I hope it's someone calling for a date."

Evi ended the call. Her mother wasn't totally wrong. Evi was terrible at dating. If she were honest with herself, she was terrible with people in general. She was extremely awkward in social situations, and she could never seem to figure out how to keep friends. The closest she ever got to having real friends was college—and that seemed like a different lifetime. None of them talked to her anymore, so that only proved that she wasn't destined to have any long-term relationships.

Evi looked at her computer monitor and felt her anxiety immediately rise. There was an error code that had been taunting her for days. Software programming was 2 percent creation and 98 percent figuring out errors. No wonder she had no friends; she spent hours looking at a monitor in a room by herself. The only people she talked to were other programmers, and it was always brief and through a computer. She was a goddess in the online gaming space, but even that had gotten old. In fact, the whole thing made her feel alone.

There was so much more to her than her ability with C++, Python, and Lua. At least, she thought so. She even tried swiping left on apps, but she often found herself staring at a wine glass as the dude across from her droned on and on about everything she couldn't care less about. She'd just nod her head, and then she wouldn't ever hear from them again. Which in itself was a mercy. She just had no idea how to talk and connect with others.

Company parties were the worst. Employees were expected to attend, make small talk, and bond as colleagues. She would rather go in for a root canal than endure an hour of handshaking and trying to remember people's names. Even though she saw them at the last uncomfortable team meeting, their names never stuck.

> *Message: Drake*
> *Evi,*
> *Where are the updates on the code for that new character? We need to be able to insert it into the beta launch in four days. If you need to take overtime, it is approved. We just need that new warrior princess to be ready for the beta testers. Done is better than perfect at this stage. The testers can send you a glitch list later.*

Fantastic. She was approved for overtime. Did they just assume she had nothing else to do? They did, and they were right. It was true she had nothing going on, but that was beyond the point. How could she have a life if she had an open overtime card?

Evi shut the computer off. She could deal with the error tomorrow. Or at 2:00 a.m. when she woke up. She would crack open an energy drink and knock it out in a couple of hours.

Her stomach rumbled. She rummaged through her fridge and realized that the magical fairies hadn't done grocery shopping. She was pretty sure the Chinese leftovers from three days before could land her in the bathroom for the next twenty-four hours. It was time to flip through some apps to pick who would be delivering food that night.

. . . . . .

The phone rang. Who would be calling after 9:00 p.m.? It wasn't a number Evi recognized. It was probably a telemarketer or a scammer. Evi was in a bickering mood, so she decided to answer, ready for a confrontation.

"Evi?" said the voice on the other end.

"How cute, you know my name. What are you selling? Or wait, let me guess. My car warranty has run—"

"Evi, it's Alex."

Evi almost dropped the phone. She scanned the room quickly for cameras. The other programmers sometimes liked to play pranks and then upload them on YouTube. If this was a prank, it wasn't a very funny one. Alex was one of Die Bande. That's what they'd called their little group of friends in college.

"If this is really Alex, what's my preference: *Star Wars* or *Star Trek*?"

There was a laugh on the other end. She could recognize that laugh anywhere. In one instant, Evi was back in the lounge with Bhavani, Desiree, Teddy, Peter, and Alex.

"The series or the movies? You loved *Star Trek*, the series, but hated the movies."

"Alex, I—what?" Evi was a real charmer when she tried.

"I'm sorry to call you so late and out of the blue like this, Evi. I hope I didn't wake anyone up, did I?"

EVERYONE IS AFRAID

It had been so long that he may have assumed she was married with a gaggle of kids.

"Did my mom put you up to this?" Evi asked with suspicion.

"What? No. I called you because . . . Well, it's been so long."

"It has," Evi admitted. "And no, you didn't wake anyone. Not even Captain."

"Captain?"

"My cat. Short for Captain Kirk. And because she is the Captain of the apartment. She's out cold on the cat tree. But I digress. How are you?"

"Not too bad, you know . . ."

The next twenty minutes of catching up was the kind Evi hated. Superficial, polite, small talk. Evi mostly let Alex talk because there was little she wanted to say.

"Sounds like a fun job. You get to play games all day," said Alex.

"It definitely sounds like it would be fun but . . . It's not all that exciting. Sure I get to try out the new games to catch any bugs, but it's tedious work on a good day."

There was a pause that seemed like it stretched for a week. If he hung up, Evi wouldn't blame him. Alex probably realized why they hadn't talked in over a decade: she wasn't a talker.

"I have to be honest, Evi," Alex said. "I didn't just call to catch up with you. I called about Teddy."

"Oh, that goofball! What has he gotten himself into now?" Evi laughed.

"Well, to get to the point, actually . . . He's dying," Alex said in a serious voice.

"He's what? OK, wait. You need to start from the beginning." For the next few minutes, Evi did what she did best: shut up and listen.

"Shit, that's terrible," Evi said after being brought up to speed. "I don't know what to say. What the hell? How?"

Evi was in a perpetual state of not knowing what to say, but this was different. Evi liked Teddy. A lot! In fact, she'd had a crush on him in college. She never had the guts to tell him, though. She was such an idiot.

"What can I do?" she asked. "I have some money put away. What am I going to do with it anyway? Leave it to Captain?"

"While I appreciate the gesture, and I'm sure he would, too, he doesn't need our money. Everyone keeps offering money. It's like they want to buy their way out of seeing their own mortality or something. Sorry. Tangent. But what he needs are his friends. He wants to see you, me, the gang. He doesn't have much time, I'm afraid."

"You weren't being dramatic, were you?" Evi replied. "He really is dying?"

"Yes, and his one request is not to die alone."

"That's pretty heavy, Alex. I mean . . . really heavy."

"I know it's a lot, Evi. Believe me. I'm having trouble facing this too. But it would mean a lot to him for us to be together again. At least one more time."

"Have you contacted the others? Surely they're coming?" Evi's anxiety was in high gear. She needed to find her special gummies after this call.

"Unfortunately, I struck out with Desiree and Bhavani. They can't make it."

Evi needed to find a way out of this conversation. There was no way she could just take off and get on a plane. She had not been on a plane in years. All those people. All those germs. No way. Captain wouldn't make a good emotional support animal. And who would take care of her if Evi was gone? And there was the glitching warrior princess that needed to be fixed. She needed to be slaying demons in four days. Nobody had time for compassion in her world.

"Alex, I . . . I can't. We're getting ready to do this big beta launch, and my character is all a mess. Hey, maybe we could do a Zoom call?"

"You mean like a business meeting teleconference?" asked Alex.

"Yeah, exactly like that. At least we can use technology to connect socially. This might be the one conference call I actually wouldn't mind being on."

"That might work. I'd need to figure out how to do that. Technical stuff isn't really my strong suit."

"I'll help set it up," Evi offered.

"So, how does it work? You come here and set it up for us?"

"Nice one, Alex," Evi said with a little chuckle. "If I could be there in person, I would. I just don't do . . . planes . . . large amounts of people . . . or . . . feelings."

"I get it," said Alex. "But maybe we could get the conference call thing to work. I'll ask the others if they could do that. It won't be the same as people coming here, but it might be better than nothing."

"I do feel bad. Please let him know I am sending him all my love." The words escaped her mouth before she could approve them.

"You want me to say that exactly?" asked Alex.

Evi felt her face flush with embarrassment. "You know what I—"

"Chill, I'm teasing you. Everyone knew you had a crush on Teddy."

Her face got even hotter. "They did? You did too? Did he know?" she asked in horror.

"Of course he did. He even tried to ask you out once, and you said you needed to get back to the computer lab."

"He asked me out?"

"Hell yeah he did, he asked if you wanted to go to dinner at Mickey's."

"Die Bande always went to Mickey's. How would I know that he meant just the two of us?"

"The way I remember, you sprinted out before he could explain anything."

The truth Evi hated to admit was that even if she'd known it was a date, she'd have been too scared or self-conscious to go.

"You know what? Yeah, tell him exactly what I said—I am sending all my love."

They hung up. Evi looked at the half-eaten pizza she had indulged in before the call. It lay there congealing in its greasy box.

She needed to change her life.

At least Teddy and Alex had each other right now. Evi had her mom and sisters, but they lived so far away. She loved them, but she didn't exactly want them to be within walking distance. What she really wanted were some friends and someone to grow old with. There, she'd admitted it. She was tired of being lonely.

EVERYONE IS AFRAID

Chapter 11:

PETER—REALTOR

Peter hung up the phone and looked around for someone to high-five, but his house was empty. How long had she been gone? Peter still expected Justine to be there to celebrate, but she wouldn't be. Not anymore. A drunk driver had made sure of that. They were supposed to grow old together. All those dreams and visions of the future were gone in an instant.

Peter had immersed himself in work so he wouldn't have to think about it. Justine wouldn't want him to sit around and wallow in his grief. Sure, he drank a little too much these days, but no one cared.

He had made three real estate deals just this week. He was on fire. But it didn't bring him joy—he had no one to share his success with anymore. Next week would have been their trip to Paris. The tickets sat on his desk. He hadn't bothered to cancel the flights. Was it denial? Did he really expect her to walk through the door like it all had been a bad dream?

Peter began scrolling through the food delivery options. Nothing sounded good. He walked over to his counter, where a mostly empty bottle of whiskey sat. He did a quick shot and then another.

"Congrats, Peter, on another deal. You sold it for ten thousand over the asking price."

Peter clanked his shot glass against the now empty bottle and drained the glass.

His phone began ringing—a number he didn't recognize. Peter looked at his watch. It wasn't too late. He was always ready to list or sell.

"Peter Jacobson."

"Peter? This is Alex."

Peter racked his brain. Did he know Alex? "I . . . uh . . ."

"Sorry, it's been a while." Alex chuckled. "This is Alex Gonzalez."

"Oh my God, Alex. How are you doing, bud?"

Peter was the party boy of their little group in college. Always up for a good time, but not always reliable. He would often promise to meet up but wouldn't, or he'd make an excuse at the last minute. If Peter found something more exciting to do, he'd cancel on his friends to do it.

Alex filled Peter in. Peter found another bottle of bourbon in the cabinet. It sat unopened as he listened to Alex's story.

"Wow, dude, that sounds horrible," Peter finally said.

"Well, I felt you should know. And . . . I was hoping you might come and see Teddy."

Another call was coming in. It was a number Peter recognized—an investor that liked flipping houses.

"Alex, listen, I need to run. I have an important call coming in."

"Sure, sure. Call me when you have a minute."

"Sure thing, bud."

The investor was looking for some new properties, and Peter agreed to show him some in the morning. He left the full bottle of bourbon alone and pulled some frozen chimichangas from the freezer. Man, did he miss Justine's cooking.

· · · · · ·

It had been almost a week since Alex had called, and business was steady, so the whole matter had slipped from Peter's radar.

"Hey, Peter," said Alex on the phone.

"Oh man, I totally flaked, Alex. I'm totally sorry."

"I get it. No problem. The reason I called you was that I wanted to know if you might want to come out to see Teddy. He isn't doing really well. I'm not sure how long he has, and his wish is not to die alone. That's why I've reached out to everyone."

A knot twisted in Peter's gut. He could see the bottle across the room, and he really needed a shot.

"I can't," Peter began. "It's not that I don't care. And it's not because I can't make the trip. It's . . . My wife died almost a year ago, and I'm still trying to deal with all that. Seeing Teddy in that state . . . I don't think I can handle it right now."

"Oh. I had no idea. I'm so sorry for your loss. I remember how head over heels you were at the wedding."

"The wedding was the last time you and I saw each other, huh? Yeah. She died in a car accident. A drunk driver. She was driving to pick up a cake for a baby shower for a friend of hers. The ER doctor said she died immediately and that she didn't suffer."

Silence hung. Peter had gotten used to that kind of silence. People didn't know what to say when he told them.

"The guy that hit her, he had no license," Peter continued. "He had it revoked for two other DUIs. He had no insurance and blew twice the legal limit. Can you believe that bastard walked away without a scratch, but my beautiful Justine—" Peter began choking up, and his hands were shaking. He tried to regain control. "We were supposed to be going to Paris this week. We didn't have a lot of money for a honeymoon, so I promised her one day I would take her to Paris. We finally saved enough, and we were going. She had made this whole itinerary—all the places she wanted to visit and eat. It was like she had every minute planned out."

Peter grabbed a tissue and blew his nose. He was a mess and wanted to end the call so he could drink and forget it. At least for a time. But he couldn't stop telling the story.

"It's funny. When she died, everyone was around. They called. They brought food. They offered prayers and flowers. And then, one by one, I stopped hearing from them. I used to be close to Justine's parents. My parents passed away a few years ago, and Justine's parents treated me like I was theirs. They insisted I call them Mom and Dad. But even they couldn't handle the shadow of Justine. I haven't heard from them in months, and I figure that might be for the best."

"I don't have anything to say," Alex replied quietly.

"You don't have to say anything. There is nothing anyone can say that will bring her back. The guy who did this made bail, and there hasn't been a trial yet. He's being charged with manslaughter. Even if they put him away forever, it won't tip the scales."

Peter's hand was shaking bad now. He needed to end the call.

"I have immersed myself in work now. I work all the time, but that isn't enough to help me forget. Every time I walk through the house, she's there. I can't explain it."

"It's OK. I don't—"

"I'm sorry, Alex. I just can't do it. I can't deal with any more death. Tell Teddy . . . Tell him . . . Tell him I love him and that I'm sorry I can't be there."

"Of course," said Alex.

"Listen, buddy, maybe we can catch up some other time. I have to go."

"I understand. You take care of yourself."

. . . . . .

Alex felt guilty hanging up the phone. Two of his friends were dealing with real issues, and he'd had no clue. He'd thought working overtime and being a partner was the most important thing. But what he was realizing was that none of that mattered.

Life could change in a second, and he needed to pay more attention to the ones he loved. Time was the one thing he couldn't get back.

Teddy wasn't feeling well and had decided to sleep instead of coming to dinner. He was eating less and less every day. It was rough on Alex, watching his friend disappear a little bit at a time. The entire situation was overwhelming.

"I can't believe it, Sheri," Alex said as he picked at his dinner. "Not one of them is coming, so far."

"You did all you could," replied Sheri as she cleared the table. Lucy was already up in her room streaming her favorite show. Steve was playing one of his online games.

"I know, but they all seemed too busy. It's like they don't care," Alex replied.

"Wait, no one said they didn't care, Alex. They have lives just like you and I do. You chose to take some time off to help Teddy, but I'll remind you that it was a very hard decision for you."

Alex had to admit she was right. He didn't like the truth, but it was what it was. He was judging people he'd had brief conversations with. He was assuming they didn't want to come and were blowing the whole thing off. If he was honest with himself, these people were virtual strangers. He had once known each of them well, but that was years ago. He had changed since college, so it was a good assumption that they had too. What he didn't know was what their stories were and what was going on for them. He realized that even though he did ask them about their lives, it was just to break the ice or make small talk. He wasn't really *hearing* them. He'd had an agenda for each call, and it was to get them to care enough to come for a visit. He had assumed they'd all drop what they were doing, just like he had.

Was he wanting them to come because he didn't want to deal with the burden and imminent pain by himself? He thought Teddy would enjoy seeing them and knowing that people still cared about him, but he had never asked Teddy if that was his wish.

After dinner, Alex checked his email. There was nothing new. He was still worried that his job was in jeopardy, and he hadn't heard anything since the meeting on Friday. He'd only gotten a brief message from Jim Conner: *Meeting went longer than expected. I will catch up with you Monday.*

· · · · · · ·

Alex had been out shopping for food and some clothes for Teddy. Lounge pants and T-shirts, mostly. This was the first time he'd had a moment to check in with Sheri. It had been almost a week since Teddy had come to stay with them, and he had quickly become a part of the family.

"How is Teddy doing?" Alex asked.

"I saw him this morning, and he didn't look so good," replied Sheri. "He was supposed to meet with someone from hospice this afternoon. He's been sleeping most of the day."

"Is he comfortable?"

"He seems to be. He doesn't seem to have much of an appetite. I told him I'd cook whatever he wanted."

Alex hesitated because he was uncomfortable with what he

was going to say next. "You know I have to go back to work next week. That is if there's any work to go back to."

"Why do you do that?" Sheri placed her hands on her hips.

"Do what?"

"Why do you always assume the worst? You said Jim told you to take the time you need. Teddy has needed you this past week, and you were there for him. Trust me, that counts for a lot. It has meant a lot to me." She took a couple of deep breaths, clearly trying not to cry.

"What's the matter?" Alex was alarmed that his wife was upset.

"I . . . I wasn't sure we were going to make it?"

"What? What do you mean?"

"You and me, Alex. You were so attached to your job. I didn't think there was room in your life for the kids and me anymore." Sheri couldn't hold it in, and a tear rolled down her cheek.

"You're leaving me?" Alex was gobsmacked.

"Hear me out. Please just listen."

Alex took a long drink of water and then a deep breath. "I'm listening."

"I have tried to tell you how unhappy we are. We miss you, Alex. You're never here, and even when you are . . . you still aren't."

Alex wanted to respond, but he willed himself to stay silent.

"I felt our lives were drifting apart. I was so afraid. To be honest, I'm still afraid. This week has been a small miracle, and now . . . Now you're going back."

"What do you mean it was a small miracle?"

"I saw the man I fell in love with, the man I married. Compassionate. Empathetic. You had a choice, and you chose to take care of your friend. I worried you would choose not to and push him off on someone else, but you didn't. I know you felt you had a lot to lose by taking time off, but you had more to lose if you didn't take the time. I was close to leaving. I admit it. But this week you have been here. Really here. Lucy and Steve have noticed too."

"What did they say?" Now it was Alex's turn to hold back his emotions.

"They love you so much, Alex. Their universe revolves around you. It has broken my heart to see them disappointed. When you missed Lucy's dance recital, when you missed Steve's science fair . . ."

"I made it up to them. I let Steve order that new online game, and I let Lucy get the overpriced stuffed animal."

"Do you think games and stuffed animals are what they want?" Sheri's impatience was plainly visible. "They don't want stuff, Alex! They want their dad! *Their daddy!* You've been here this week and have actually spent some time with them. Tonight when Lucy took her bath, she told me how happy she was. Daddy was home, and she couldn't wait until you read the next chapter in her book to her."

Alex's eyes stung from the tears welling up in them. "I . . . I don't know what to say," he admitted.

"When you tell me that you're going back to work next week, it scares me."

Alex got up from the table, walked over to his wife, and

embraced her. He could feel hot tears on his cheeks and neck. He wasn't sure if they were hers or his.

"I had no idea. I've been so focused on becoming a partner that I guess I've become obsessed. I've been neglecting everything else that matters to us."

Sheri laughed. "You think?"

"I was so scared at work. Everything I was trying at work didn't work. I'd produce project miracles and I'd get the privilege of producing more project miracles. The only thing I could think of was to work harder and longer. I was trading off time now for time later. What I wasn't seeing was all the consequences of the trade-offs. And I had to figure it out on my own because asking for help—heck, even being open to help—was a sign of vulnerability and weakness."

Alex held his wife at arm's length and looked her directly in her eyes. "One thing I am coming to terms with is that there are things in life much more important than being able to figure it out on my own. There are trade-offs at home I will not make any more, and I think there are trade-offs at work I will not make anymore. I don't want to end up like Teddy, alone and with regret. I love you, Sheri, and I promise you—promise *you*—I will not go back to the way things were. I'm not sure how I'll do it, and you might have to be patient with me as I figure out how to accept help, but now I get why you and the kids want me to be home more. And why that would be good for me too. Maybe it means I have to find new employment. I do know, that I do not know."

Sheri kissed her husband deeply. "I love you, Alex."

"I love you too."

"I'm confused," said Lucy. She was standing in the doorway of the kitchen in her PJs, ready for bed. "You're hugging and crying. Are you happy or sad?"

"Both!" said Sheri and Alex at the same time.

"Get over here," said Alex. Lucy ran and was crushed between her parents as they hugged.

Alex knew that something had changed at that moment. He realized he had not been listening to his daughter, his son, his wife, or even his life. He had only been listening to the voice in his head and assuming that they also wanted him to become a partner and bring home more money. Now he could tell that wasn't working. All they wanted was for him to be present.

Alex didn't plan on calling and quitting, but he did need to have a serious discussion with Jim. Things would have to change, and he hoped that Jim would understand. He might never make partner, but he was OK with that as long as he had his family. That was all that mattered.

"Uh, Dad. Dad, you're crushing me."

Everyone laughed. Alex knew that as long as he listened and asked his family what they wanted, he wouldn't ever be in danger of losing them again.

EVERYONE IS AFRAID

Chapter 12:

IT'S TIME

Nothing good happens after 11:00 p.m., Alex's mom used to say.

"Alex. Alex, wake up," said Sheri as she gently nudged her husband. Alex rolled over; it was 2:00 a.m.

"What's going on?" Alex asked.

"The hospice nurse called 911. The ambulance is on the way."

It had been three weeks since Teddy came to live with them, and there had been hospice care to help them out. At least to get a little sleep. Teddy needed constant care and couldn't leave the bed. He didn't want to go to the hospital, so they set up a hospital bed in the dining room because there was a door that could be closed. Alex had known this moment was coming, but he still felt vastly unprepared.

"What happened?" Alex asked.

"Teddy stopped breathing. I think it's time." Tears rolled down Sheri's cheek.

"I'll get up. Can you stay with the kids?"

"Of course."

. . . . . .

Alex could barely keep his eyes open. He drank a lot of coffee in the past hour, and it made his stomach sour.

A nurse came out to the waiting room and walked toward him. "Are you Alex?" she asked.

"Yes."

"Can you please come back with me?"

Instead of going to where Teddy was, they went to a room.

"Wait here a moment. The doctor will be right in," the nurse said as she closed the door.

Alex knew it wasn't going to be good news. It was Teddy's time, and Alex tried to prepare himself for it.

A doctor entered with a very somber look on her face. "Are you Alex Gonzalez?"

"Yes."

"Are you related to Teddy Morganston?" she asked as she flipped through a chart.

"No. I'm just a good friend of his."

Alex felt a pang of guilt saying that. He had been anything but a good friend. He wasn't sure that three weeks made up for years of no contact with Teddy.

"He passed peacefully. Is there anyone else you'd like me to contact? Family? He didn't list anyone else except you."

That last statement was a blow. Alex had met Teddy's parents when they were in college. He knew they were still living in the same house. He still had their number somewhere to call them. He didn't have the number for Teddy's estranged wife, but perhaps Judy, Teddy's mother, would have it.

"He wasn't close to his family. I know how to get in touch with them." Alex could feel a lump in his throat, and he was holding back tears he had not expected.

"Of course," the doctor said. "And I'm sorry for your loss."

As Alex drove home through the nearly empty predawn streets, he thought about Teddy and his life. He tried to formulate what he would say to his family. He was coming up short. He had heard Teddy's story, and it was obvious there was a lot of pain when it came to his family. Alex only hoped that whatever their differences were, Teddy's parents would put them aside in the face of this loss. Or that at least they would want to know.

The house was quiet. Maybe Sheri and the kids had fallen back asleep. It was too early to begin calling people, so Alex began making lists of who to call and what arrangements would need to be made. He had promised he would take care of everything when this day came. Teddy had been resistant at first, but then he'd thanked his friend with tears and a hug.

· · · · · ·

"Judy?"

"Yes?"

"Judy, this is Alex Gonzalez. I was friends with your son in college. I spent a few weekends at your home."

"Alex—yes, of course, I remember you. How are you doing? It's been a long time."

"Yes, it has."

"Well, if you're trying to get ahold of Teddy . . . eh . . . I can't help you. We haven't heard from him in about a year."

This was going to be hard. But Alex was committed. "As a matter of fact, I'm calling about him. I've been with him the past few weeks."

"Oh?"

"I'm afraid I have some bad news. Your son was very ill. He had terminal cancer, and at about one o'clock this morning . . . he died."

Judy gulped. "Fred!" she shouted. "Fred, get in here!"

There were some muffled words that Alex couldn't quite make out.

"Alex, I have my husband Fred here," Judy said, her voice cracking. "Are you sure? Are you sure our son is . . . gone?"

Alex took a deep breath. He wanted to hold it together. It was going to be a long day. He needed to push through his feelings and be present for Teddy.

"Yes, he is gone," Alex replied. He noticed how he could not say Teddy's name. If he did, he would not be able to stop crying.

"Alex, this is Fred, Ted's dad," said a male voice. "We . . . we have not seen our son in some time. We were always afraid this day would come. This call. Fuck."

"Fred, please," said Judy.

"We knew he had lost his job, and then his wife left him," continued Fred. "He stayed with us for a bit, but when the drinking got bad, we couldn't help him. He didn't want to be helped. He was too far gone."

"I understand," Alex replied.

"We love our son, Alex," added Judy. "He just wouldn't listen to us. He was so hurt by his wife leaving and losing his job. We knew he was sick, but he wouldn't go to the doctor."

There was silence, and Alex allowed it. He didn't want to jump in. He wanted to give them space.

"Did he suffer?" asked Fred.

Alex thought about the question. Teddy had suffered because he was alienated from everyone. Alex hoped that he had provided him a little bit of comfort in his final days.

"Because of his illness? No, he didn't suffer that much," Alex replied. "Hospice was with him and kept him comfortable. From what they told me, he passed in his sleep. He never woke up. But he was lonely."

Alex could hear Judy sobbing now.

"It's OK, dear," said Fred. "Why don't you get us some tea, and I'll talk to Alex." There was a pause. Then Fred spoke again. "This has been especially hard on Judy. She hasn't slept worrying about where he was. How did you find him?"

Alex told the whole story. He regretted telling it after it was out because he didn't want to cause Fred or Judy any further pain.

"Thank you, Alex, for sharing that," said Fred. "Truly, I can't thank you enough. That Ted was not alone means so much to me."

Alex didn't know how to respond.

"We, of course, will take care of all the funeral arrangements. We have the house over on Lake Geneva in Wisconsin. We can have a memorial there. There's a family plot in upstate New York. We can have a small service there and then a bigger get-together. Since we're over here on the East Coast, can you help with opening up the lake house and see if it needs anything before guests arrive? I understand if you decline— you've done so much already."

"I'd be honored to help," Alex replied.

"Again, thank you. Let me check on Judy, and we'll call and make some more arrangements later this afternoon."

"Of course," Alex said. "Take your time."

As they hung up, Alex felt like a burden had been lifted from his heart. Even though Teddy had parted from his family, they would be getting together to celebrate his life. Alex needed to call his German club friends next. Perhaps they could come early and help him with the house. And perhaps they could finally reconnect.

Chapter 13:

TIME OFF

Alex had gone to bed early. It was so much to deal with, and with the lack of sleep, he was exhausted. The phone woke him—it was ten o'clock in the morning. He missed picking it up before it was too late. He figured it was probably the office calling. He was sure Jim Conner was furious that Alex wasn't in the office yet. Alex still needed to get up to speed on the new client, but with Teddy's passing, he was an emotional mess. He needed to pull himself together and focus.

Even though he wanted to stay home for another week, there was no reason to. Teddy was gone, and his parents were taking care of the service. It would be a few weeks until Alex needed to go to the lake house in preparation for the memorial. In the meantime, he needed to return to work. Despite his previous promise that things would be different going forward,

Sheri wasn't happy with his decision. Alex didn't have the energy to argue with her. He promised that he would come home at a decent time, even though, in his heart, he wasn't sure he could make good on the promise.

Alex was getting dressed when the phone rang again.

"Hey, I know I'm late," he began, not even bothering to see who the caller was. "Something happened yesterday, and I—"

"Hello? Is this Alex?"

Alex was confused. It wasn't a voice that he recognized.

"I am so sorry. Yes, this is Alex." He took a quick peek at the phone. It was a Boston area code, but he wasn't familiar with the number. The identity said *unknown*. Great, it was probably a telemarketer. "Listen, I'm late for an appointment, so—"

"I'm sorry to bother you," said the female voice. She was talking softly, and it almost sounded like she was crying.

Alex softened his tone. "I'm sorry—who is this?"

"This is Julie Brooks. I'm Teddy's wife. Well, ex. I'm not sure."

"Oh no. Mrs. Brooks, I'm so sorry," Alex said.

"It's fine, you can call me Julie. I know we've never met, but I do feel like I know you. Teddy didn't talk much about his past, but he did mention you and some German club from school. He said you were the only real friends he ever had."

Alex didn't know how to respond. If he heard Julie cry again, he might start crying. He took a deep breath.

"I don't know about that, but yeah, we were all good friends."

"I got a call from Fred and Judy last night. Even though Teddy and I weren't living together, we stayed in touch. They had nothing but wonderful things to say about you and how you helped Teddy at . . . at the end."

"He, ah . . . said he really missed you and the kids. And that he was really sorry about the way things happened, and . . ."

"Alex, when I last saw my husband, he wasn't the same man I knew. He was consumed with work, and then the alcohol, and . . . there just wasn't room for me and the kids in his life anymore. I begged him to get help, but he wouldn't listen. I tried to reach out to him about the being sick, but he wouldn't respond. I never ever stopped loving him, Alex. Never. We just couldn't make it together anymore."

Julie was sobbing now. Alex felt his own eyes well up. Teddy's life had gone so wrong, and he just didn't see what a mess he had made of it until the end. Alex was sure his parents and his wife would have forgiven him. The problem was Teddy couldn't forgive himself. And now, it was too late.

"I can tell you, he loved you and the girls too. He was holding on to a lot of guilt, and he didn't want his kids to see him in the condition he was in. He didn't want to cause any of you any pain. I tried to get him to reach out to you, to his parents, to any of his friends, but he didn't want to. I even called our old friends to see if they could come and see him because I didn't want him to feel alone, but all of them were too busy."

"I'm sorry to hear that," Julie responded between sniffles.

"Oh, I don't want to upset you," Alex said. Now he felt like a jerk telling her all these things.

"No, I can't tell you how relieved I am to hear that he connected with you and that you helped him. As I said, he'd mention you and your friends from time to time, but when I asked him to call or look you up, he always brushed it off. He was either too busy or he thought you all were too busy and wouldn't call him back."

Alex had to admit that Teddy might have been right. With work and his pursuit of partnership in the firm, Alex didn't allow any "distractions." At least, that was the case a few weeks ago. Alex had thought his goals were so important. Now, none of them were important. His family and friends needed to be his new priority if he wanted to live without regrets.

Alex didn't know what Julie wanted or needed from him at that moment. He wanted the call to end because it was awkward and painful. He was sure anything he said would only upset Julie further.

"Is there anything I can do for you, Julie?" he finally asked. "Fred offered to have a memorial at their lake house. I was going to call our friends again to see if they could come. But if you'd rather handle that, I would totally respect your wishes."

"Alex, I wouldn't think of it. You and your friends should get together. I'm going to have my hands full with the kids and the estate. I haven't told the girls yet. Even though they haven't seen him in a while, they ask about him every day. This is going to break their hearts. Again."

More sobs. Alex couldn't fathom the depth of pain Julie was experiencing.

"I'm sorry. Well, uh, you have my number. Please call me anytime. And don't worry, I'll touch base with Fred and Judy and help out with the funeral arrangements."

There were some more sniffles on the line. Then a deep breath.

"Thank you, Alex."

.   .   .   .   .   .

Alex couldn't make it in. He called his assistant and let him know he was dealing with Teddy's death. He asked him to pass on the information to Jim.

But Alex couldn't just sit at home; it wasn't in his nature. He finished getting dressed and decided to go into the city to clear his head a bit. The first stop was to get some of Harriet's coffee. He hadn't had any in a few weeks. He had missed the coffee, and honestly, he missed chatting with Harriet.

"You want your usual?" asked Harriet as Alex sat down at the counter. There was so much floating around his head. He was still processing Teddy's death and talking to his family. He knew he needed to speak with their friends, but he was having a hard time just mustering up the will to call them. It really seemed like they didn't care, but in his heart, he knew that wasn't true. It couldn't be true.

"Yes, please." It was after the morning rush, and so the shop was mostly empty. The silence and lack of chaos were a blessing.

"You're here at a strange hour," Harriet observed. "How is that friend of yours doing?"

Alex stared at the espresso machine. "He died, actually."

Harriet's eyes went wide. "Well, I'm sorry to hear that. How are you holding up?" she asked as the steaming wand hissed.

"I guess . . . I knew Teddy's time was limited," Alex said.

"I just didn't know it was going to be so soon."

"Do you want to talk about it?"

"Yes, please. I don't know what to say. I talked to his parents and his wife, and that was . . . difficult."

"You are a good man and a great friend."

"Am I though?" Alex asked. "Where was I the last decade? I never looked him up. I never called."

"Do you think things would be different now?" Harriet asked. "Would reaching out to him stop his cancer?"

Alex had to think about that. He accepted the coffee and blew on it. He wasn't used to it being in an actual mug rather than a paper cup.

"I suppose not," he admitted. "I just hate that he died without his family being there."

"But *you* were there," said Harriet. "And that meant something to him."

"Really? You think so?"

"I have watched you come into my shop for years. Your phone to your ear or a stare that's a million miles away. You were so focused on your work that I dared not try to break your concentration. When you were present, you always smiled and were generous. That's how I know you're a good person, Alex. You might have been distracted by many other things in your life, but on the inside, you are generous and kind, and you proved that by helping your friend. I hope you're not going to go back to hiding that good person."

Alex sat silent for a few minutes, sipping his coffee. In his head, he had painted a picture: saving Teddy from losing his family, finding him a job, helping him beat cancer. But that was all a story he was making up in his head. And because of that bogus story, Alex was beating himself up for failing to save Teddy. The truth was that Alex was living his life like Teddy had lived his. Alex was hurting the people he cared about just like Teddy had. But Alex was the lucky one. He still had time to change.

"I am honored to have been there for him, and being there for Teddy has been a tipping point for me. You're right," Alex said.

"Of course I am, honey." Harriet laughed. "I'm brilliant!"

Alex had to laugh too. Wow, how long had it been since he'd laughed? It felt both foreign and natural.

"My point is, you are being too hard on yourself," said Harriet. "I don't know too many people that would have done what you did for him. You made a broken man feel like someone cared for him in this world. And these days, we could all use a bit of that."

"Thank you."

"You need to take care of yourself. Promise me you will."

"Oh, this whole experience has changed me," Alex replied. "It has rewritten many of the stories in my head. In fact, I wanted to tell you how much I appreciate you. Not just recently but every day. You always meet me with a smile in the morning, and I feel that I have never shared with you until now how that has set my day right on so many occasions."

Alex reached into his jacket pocket and slipped an envelope to Harriet.

"What's this?" she asked.

"I'll probably be gone for the remainder of the month, with

the memorial service and all. I wanted to give you something as a token of my appreciation since I won't be buying coffee."

"Oh, Alex, you didn't have to give me anything. It's always been my pleasure," replied Harriet.

"I know. Will you let me do this for both of us? You can open it now."

Harriet walked around the counter. "Can I give you a hug?"

"Yeah, but you don't have to . . ."

Harriet gave Alex a hug that lasted long enough to make him feel connected.

"You're right," she replied. "I don't have to. I want to. Thank you!"

. . . . . .

Alex had another stop he wanted to make before he headed home.

"Hey, busy man," said Harry. "What's the news? I haven't seen you in a while. Everything OK?"

Harry was a second-generation American. His family was from Albania. He was hardworking and no matter the weather, he always had his newsstand open. The only time someone else was working the stand was when his sister was sick and when his uncle died. Alex knew all of this because every time he'd come across someone new there, he'd felt compelled to ask if Harry was OK—even though he'd rarely taken the time to talk to Harry himself. Most of the time, apparently, Harry was off for soccer. His family were fanatics. Everyone played—his kids, his siblings, and even Harry himself in a local men's club.

"Yeah, I had a friend that was sick, and he passed away," Alex replied.

"Oh no. I am so sorry to hear that," said Harry. "Is there anything I can do for you?"

That caught Alex off guard. He only bought newspapers from Harry. Sure, they saw each other most mornings, but Alex was always in a rush to get to the office before anyone else, so they'd never really talked.

"Well, thank you, Harry," Alex said. "That is very generous."

"Tell me the address," continued Harry. "My wife will kill me if I don't get your address."

"What do you mean?"

"It's what my family does. Whenever someone dies, or someone is sick, we bring food to people. Even if they're a neighbor we don't really know. We do it to support people in their time of grief and need. You've been such a great customer for years, and I mention you to my wife. You're a funny man and kind of a local fixture, even if you don't know it." He winked. "And your name is Alex, right?"

"How did you know?"

"Harriet and I talk."

"Ah, of course." Alex smiled. "Well, that is very generous of you. I'll be leaving town for a week or so, though, so I won't be home."

"Oh, well, can we at least send some flowers to brighten up your house?"

Alex felt that if he turned him down, it might hurt Harry's feelings. "Sure, that would be fine. My wife loves flowers," he replied, and he gave Harry his address. "I really stopped by to give you this, though." Alex handed him an envelope like the one he'd given Harriet.

"What is this?" Harry asked with a frown.

"It's just something to show my thanks and appreciation. Since I won't be by for a while to get my usual paper."

"Oh, that's very nice of you."

"You've brightened my day many times, Harry. I know it probably doesn't seem like it since I'm always in a rush, but it's meant a lot, just knowing you're here when I come to get my paper. You help get my day going. I trust you more than I trust the news stations."

They both chuckled.

"Listen," said Harry. "I've actually been waiting for you to come back in. My cousin owns a conglomerate of newspapers and magazines around the country. He was talking the other day about expanding his holdings and he said he was looking for a new firm to work with. You work at a law firm, right? Do you mind if I have him call you? His company is the Theseus Media Group. Have you heard of it?"

Of course Alex had! They were the third-largest media company in the country.

"That would be great," Alex replied, astonished. It would be a huge asset for the firm and one that would continue to grow over time.

"Maybe when you're back in town, the three of us can have dinner together?"

"Yes, that would be wonderful."

EVERYONE IS AFRAID

Alex was amazed by his luck. Or was it luck? He'd always heard that the key to success wasn't what you know but who you know. Alex was just curious about the timing. This was the first proper conversation he'd had with Harry, after all.

"I need to get home," Alex said. "Tomorrow I'll be back to settle my office for a bit before I take off some time. I'll come by and say hi."

"It was great seeing you, Alex. I am very sorry for your loss." Harry clapped Alex on the back.

"I appreciate it."

Harry hesitated for a moment. "You know, I see a lot of businessmen here every day. Why don't you leave some of your cards with me, and I'll send some more business your way. You have a good heart, Alex, I can tell. And Harriet can tell. I would feel great referring you."

Alex reached into his wallet and handed the few cards he had to Harry. "I can't thank you enough. If you ever need more, let me know."

"Of course," Harry said. "The best of luck, and you stay safe."

Alex reflected on how many other times people may have offered him help. He wondered about the times he was too focused to notice it, and he cringed over the times he'd even been insulted by it.

. . . . . .

The next morning Alex got up early.

"Are you sure you want to do this?" asked Sheri.

"Yes. I'm sorry about all the arguments. You were right."

"Can you speak up a little louder for the microphone," Sheri said with a wink as she sipped her favorite tea.

"Seriously. This thing with Teddy hit me, us, harder than I thought it would. I have to let go of my crusade to be partner."

Sheri kissed her husband. "I love you!"

"I love you too."

In his mind, Alex rehearsed what he would say to Jim. He hoped Jim would be as accommodating as he had been when Alex took time off to care for Teddy.

"How are you doing, Alex?" asked Jim as he escorted Alex into his office. Jim and the rest of the firm had been so supportive and understanding over the last few weeks. Being a pessimist, Alex was ready for the other shoe to drop.

"I'm doing OK," Alex said. "As I told you on the phone, my friend Teddy has passed away, and there's a lot I've had to deal with and take care of."

"I know you had been close to him these past few weeks, so my condolences. Drink?"

"I'll pass for the moment. I need to get some of my work done before I go. I wanted to come in person and ask you about taking some more time off. I need about three weeks to help with the memorial service and then to take some time with my family."

Alex held his breath. Until Teddy, he had never really asked for time off, and now he was asking for another three weeks off.

Jim seemed lost in thought, and Alex immediately regretted asking. He needed to fix this—quick.

"Well, I guess I don't need to take off that much time," Alex began.

"The time isn't the issue," said Jim, holding up a hand. "Of course you can have the time. I just didn't think I'd ever hear *you* ask for it. You've had your nose to the grindstone so much that I believed you would burn out or quit. It's one of the reasons we've been reluctant to offer you a partnership. We didn't believe you would survive burnout."

"Really?" Alex was stunned.

"Yes, and we also didn't believe you would trust others here at the firm to take over any of your work. But you trusted Todd to handle the contract closing and to work on some other cases. That's the type of person we want as a partner. Someone who *wants* to be a partner and share in the work we do."

Alex felt time slow down. Had he been that wrong? He'd thought he had to do it all on his own and not let anyone else help. He had made up a story in his head that he needed to prove to everyone that he could do it alone, without anyone's help, and that if he delegated, people would take the credit for his hard work. Maybe it was simpler than that. Accepting help meant everyone would know he was not enough. That was his real fear: not being enough.

"You take the time you need. When you get back, let's talk about transitioning you to a partner position. I've talked to the other partners, and we are all in agreement." Jim held out his hand. "Congratulations. And don't worry. Todd and some of the others are prepared to cover your cases while you're gone. Take time off and spend it with your friends and family."

Alex had a lump in his throat. He realized being more vulnerable and trusting others made the whole partnership stronger. His first thought was to share this with Sheri. His second thought was about how he could share what he'd discovered with others in a way they could hear. He was pretty sure if someone had told him this a few months ago, he would not have listened.

Chapter 14:

IT'S WHAT THE DOCTOR ORDERED

Finally, Bhavani was able to take a break. She was exhausted. The number of people coming in with the new virus was simply overwhelming. This virus was deadly and spreading quickly. Many fingers were being pointed to where it started and whose fault it was, but none of that mattered now. People were unable to breathe, and Bhavani had seen two fatalities in the past week.

She debated the safety of going home, even though she took every precaution in the world. At least she could test herself for the virus, which she often did, as she had to treat so many people every shift. Some days she had to work back-to-back shifts, and often had to ask what day it was because they all seemed to blur together. At least there was a room to sleep in for those working long hours. But who was she fooling? She could hardly rest; she felt selfish for taking the time to leave the ER.

The head of the department was concerned and pulled her aside. "Bhavani, you need to take time off, *now*. Don't come in tomorrow unless I call you."

"But we're already short-staffed. We're swamped."

"You aren't going to do anyone any good if you get sick," her boss said. "You can't work any more doubles. It's not safe for you or the patients. You need to go home and rest for a few days."

"But—"

"But nothing," her boss replied with her hands on her hips. "I'm not asking. I am telling you."

So here she was at home, taking her prescribed break.

Bhavani looked at her phone. Four missed calls and six messages, all from the same number: Alex's. It wasn't going to be good news. Since Alex had first called, Bhavani couldn't get Teddy out of her mind.

Bhavani's boss wasn't the only person who'd been insisting she take a few days' break. Her husband had been asking her to as well. He was afraid she was going to burn out, but he just didn't understand that she was essential right now. She couldn't just take off—not to see a sick friend, not for any other reason. She had to be here to treat people, and with this new pandemic, she needed to be present. Who knew how bad it could get?

On the other hand, Bhavani couldn't ignore a friend needing help. Wouldn't she be hypocritical if she only offered support to strangers? Even though they hadn't talked in a long time, Teddy was still her friend.

"Hey, Bhavani," said Alex when he answered the phone.

"I'm sorry I didn't call back sooner," she replied. "It's been a crazy few weeks, and it's not getting better."

"I'm sorry, I can only imagine. I have some rather bad news. Teddy passed away."

Bhavani inhaled quickly and dabbed at the sides of her eyes, surprised to feel tears. She saw death every day, she was always moved by the news of someone's passing. This was different, however. This was someone she knew—and worse, she had regrets. She had put off seeing him, and now it was too late.

"I'm so sorry . . . I . . . I don't know what else to say." Bhavani sat down hard on the bed. Her heart was racing, and an ache was creeping into her chest.

"I know this is difficult news," said Alex in a calm voice. She supposed Alex had more time to process what was going on, and at least he had been there for their friend.

"Is there going to be a funeral?"

"Yes, but it's for close family mostly," said Alex.

Bhavani realized she knew little about Teddy and his family. "Is there somewhere I can send flowers or at least a card to the family?"

"Yes, I can text that to you," said Alex. "One of the reasons I'm calling is that there will be a memorial service at his family's cabin on Lake Geneva. I wanted to invite you. In fact, I'm inviting everyone from German club."

"I remember that place," she said. "We all spent a spring break there our junior year. Who else is coming?"

"You're the first person I called."

It would be great to see everyone. She did miss the group and did regret not staying in touch, but life had a way of pulling people away from things. Getting through med school was no picnic, and now she had a young family. Her responsibilities overshadowed any consideration of a social life or keeping up with friends. Whenever she thought about her friends, her next thought was always that she should look them up and give them a call soon. The problem was that "soon" never came.

She was out of time, and she would never see or talk to Teddy again. That was difficult for Bhavani to swallow. Sadness felt heavy in her heart.

"Are you still there?" asked Alex.

"Yeah, this is just . . . such a shock. I should've known better. It was terminal cancer. Intellectually I knew he didn't have a long time. Still . . . I thought he had more time. It's stupid, I know."

"You're not stupid, Bhavani. I felt the same way, and suddenly he was gone. It's why I'd like us all to reconnect. I don't want to have someone else die and feel like I didn't have time for them. This experience has really changed my perspective on what is important in my life. I'm afraid if I hadn't found Teddy, he would have died alone on the streets. This has been a wake-up call for me."

Bhavani didn't want to break down on the phone. She had to end the call.

"Listen, Alex, I need to go. Let me just think about it, and I'll get back to you."

"OK," said Alex. "I really hope you can make it. I'll text you the details later today."

As she hung up the phone, Bhavani was torn. On the one hand, she really wanted to check out of her life, or what it had become, and go see her friends and reconnect. But on the other hand, she couldn't see a way to do it. With the kids and her work, she just couldn't get away. Even though her boss had told her to stay home, Bhavani knew she'd get the call to come in tomorrow. They were overwhelmed.

Frank walked into the bedroom with a strange look on his face. "What's my wife doing home at a reasonable hour?" he joked.

"Hey, honey. I came home early. Nancy said I was working too much if you can believe that."

"I can believe it, and I'm glad they insisted." Frank stepped closer. "Are you crying?"

Bhavani reached up to her face instinctively, and her cheek was wet with tears. She hadn't realized she was still crying. "Oh, it's nothing."

"No, no—it's something because I rarely see you cry. You gave birth to two kids without any pain meds and never shed a tear. Spill it."

She sighed. "I just got a call that a close friend from college passed away. You know I haven't kept up with my friends from college. You know how it is."

With downcast eyes, Frank nodded. "I do. I'm sorry for you, honey."

"I hadn't seen or talked to my friend Teddy for years. I don't know why I'm crying. I'm just exhausted and sad for him, for this whole situation."

"Bhavani, you are a human. I've seen you work day in and day out without getting upset. You do the job better than any doctor there, but sometimes I worry about how you do it without it affecting you. If it's all bottled up inside you, I'm afraid of what will become of you when it finally comes out. "

"It affects me, but I don't have time to deal with it. None of us do, really. There's always another patient waiting for us out there, all the time. Accidents and emergencies don't take days off."

"Is there going to be a funeral?"

"Yes, but it's just going to be close family there. They're going to have a bigger memorial service, I think, next week at Lake Geneva."

"You're going, of course," said Frank. It was more of a statement than a question.

"I don't . . . I really can't take off work," Bhavani said.

"Bhavani, I believe in you and everything you do. Med school, ER work, double shifts, working days straight, coming home exhausted, having kids and being a wife on top of it all. Part of my promise to you was to cherish you. You know that I hold what you care about as what I care about. I can't *not* cherish you. I can't stand by and let you *not* go to your friend's memorial when I see his death bringing you to tears. We all have our limits, Bhavani, and you have reached yours. Whether it's the passing of your friend or burnout, I cannot stand by anymore and not keep my promise. I will take care of everything here. I will even keep the kitchen clean."

Bhavani surrendered. Tears flowed and she felt herself fall into Frank's arms. She was lucky to have the love of someone who really got her.

EVERYONE IS AFRAID

Chapter 15:

THE CAR HAS TO GO

"Our guys are all done with their assessment, Desiree," said Pete, the finance guy at Easy Car Sales. "Here's your quote. If it looks good, we can get you a check today."

Pete had a glued-on smile that was fraying Desiree's nerves, but she needed to get her car sold today. What was left of her staff was ready to walk out, and their office landlord had threatened eviction if she couldn't come up with the full month's rent before five o'clock. It was already after three, and this was her last chance. She hadn't even planned how to get back to the office. She knew if she called Kate, she would get a long lecture.

Desiree looked at the paper and almost choked. "That's all? There's not even twenty thousand miles on that car, and I paid almost twice that at the dealership."

"You know what they say. Once you drive the car off the lot, it begins to depreciate," said Pete with his annoying grin.

"But not that much," she replied. "Can't you do better? That is way below Kelley Blue Book."

"Sorry, you have a car that isn't easy to sell, and we might take a loss on it. We're really doing you a favor here."

Desiree's face grew hot as she tried to control her temper. She hated being condescended to, and she knew full well that the dealership would make a tidy profit. Pete must have smelled the desperation on her and was taking advantage of the situation. She looked at her watch; she was running out of time.

"Fine, but I'll need that money in a cashier's check or deposited into my account today," she said. She caught a faint passing smile on Pete's face, which only infuriated her. "In addition, I'll need someone to run me to my office when we're done. I have a business to take care of, so time is crucial."

"I'll see what we can do," said Pete. He wasn't even trying to hide his smugness as he left her sitting in the waiting room.

Desiree's phone rang. It was Alex. Again? Could this day get any better?

"Alex, I'm sorry," she said as she answered the phone. "Now is not a great time. I'm selling my car at the moment."

"Teddy's dead," said Alex in a monotone voice.

"Wait, what?" She sat straight in her chair.

"He died a few days ago. There's been a lot going on with arrangements, and I'm sorry that I couldn't connect to let you know sooner."

Desiree was struck speechless. She had been so busy trying

to keep her life afloat that she had completely forgotten about Teddy being sick. Now it all came rushing back to her. She had intended to see Teddy once things had settled, but now it was too late. Teddy was gone.

Desiree stepped outside the small dealership office because she didn't want Pete to see her crying. He would think it was about her car, and she didn't want to give him the satisfaction of breaking her.

"I . . . I . . . I've been so caught up in work, there just wasn't any good time to come out to see him."

"I get it, I really do," replied Alex. "Listen, one of the reasons I called was to let you know that the gang is getting together at Teddy's parents' cabin on Lake Geneva."

"Oh wow, I loved that place," she replied. She wiped away tears as they flowed from her eyes. This was the worst day ever.

"Do you think you might make it? It would mean a lot," asked Alex.

Her stomach knotted.

"Alex, I wish I could. Things are a bit of a mess here. I'm selling my car in order to try to save my business as we speak."

"Oh, Desiree, I'm so sorry to hear that. Is there anything I can do?"

"That is very generous of you," she said. "I just have to get some money flowing again."

"No explanation needed. You'll be missed. I'll send you the information, just in case you can make it."

.   .   .   .   .   .

"There you are," said Kate when Desiree entered the office. "I've been trying to reach you all morning."

It didn't bode well that Kate was waiting to talk to her. Desiree worried Kate knew she had sold her car. The good news was she had deposited the check. She might have to tighten her belt for a couple of weeks, but she believed they would make it.

"Oh?" Desiree replied. "I had some errands this morning. I have good news."

"Well, I have some great news," Kate said with a big smile.

"You go first," Desiree said. The fact that Kate was smiling was amazing considering she hadn't been for weeks.

"Remember when you were going to have that meeting with the people at Miratomi Plaza?"

"Yeah? They left before I could get back," Desiree said. "I haven't heard from them, so I assume they found someone else."

"I have a confession to make. I took the meeting," said Kate in a rush.

"You what?"

"I know you told me to delay them, but they weren't going to wait around. So, I pitched them our services."

Desiree didn't know whether to be mad at Kate or thrilled that she'd taken the initiative.

"Why didn't you tell me?"

"You've been so stressed lately, and it's been hard to communicate with you, honestly. I wanted to wait until it was good news," Kate replied.

"And?"

"They called today. Not only do they want us to clean the offices in their building, but they also have other properties around the city. In addition, they're requesting we do some extra disinfecting to deal with the virus that's been spreading."

"That's amazing, but we don't have the equipment to do that," Desiree replied.

"That's the best part. They're willing to fund buying the special gear we'll need, and they're willing to pay our fees four months in advance. They know we'll need to hire more people, and so they want to make sure we have the means to do it. They want us to start in a couple of weeks."

Desiree was crying again. But this time, they were tears of relief and joy. Not only were they going to be able to save the business, but they also had an opportunity to grow. Desiree sat down and fished out a tissue from her bag.

"Are you OK?" Kate asked.

"Not really, but don't mind me," Desiree replied. "It's been a really long day."

"So, what's your good news?"

"It's kind of silly now."

"Come on . . ."

"I sold my car."

"That doesn't sound silly," Kate said. "I never thought that car fit your personality. So what kind of car did you get?"'

"That's the thing. I sold it to get enough money to keep the office open. I deposited the funds on the way here. Surprise. I saved the day. Or today, at least." Desiree laughed nervously. Kate had saved them all, and Desiree felt terrible that she hadn't trusted her more. Kate was more than capable, but Desiree felt like she had to fix everything on her own.

"Oh no, Desiree. What are you going to do? We could take that money now and buy another car."

"Yeah, I guess you're right. I need to get something a bit more practical. I can't tell you how happy I am to hear that news. Today was a tough day."

"What else happened?" asked Kate as she found Desiree another tissue.

"Remember I told you my friend Teddy was sick? I hoped I could visit after all this mess was worked out, but . . ." Desiree took a few breaths. The weight of the day and the loss of her friend overwhelmed her emotions. "I got a call today. Teddy passed away.".

"Oh, sweetie, that's terrible news. I am so sorry to hear that," said Kate. She walked over to Desiree and gave her friend a big hug. "So, are you going to the funeral?"

"I don't think there is one, or at least Alex didn't mention it. He did say our old gang from school was getting together at a cabin for the memorial."

"You know," said Kate. "That might be exactly what you need. I can handle things here."

Desiree's initial impulse was to say no because of all the work that needed to be done: hire and onboard new employees, learn to use the new machines, and get the business flowing again. Then she stopped herself. She had always believed she needed to be on hand all the time to ensure things were done and to put out any fires. The result was that she was beginning to burn out. Kate had handled the new clients like a champ, and Desiree needed to trust her more.

"Are you sure?" she asked.

"Of course I am," said Kate. "I've got this, and if I need help, I know you're a phone call away. You need this."

"I need this," Desiree echoed, and she meant it. "Oh, one last thing."

"Sure."

"Can you give me a ride home?"

EVERYONE IS AFRAID

Chapter 16:

GAME OVER

"Did you see it?"

Evi was trying to watch the gamer stream and talk to Linda at the same time, but she was struggling. "Just a sec," Evi said into her microphone. "I'm trying to watch."

"Butter Bear loves your warrior princess. He's going on and on about how it's his favorite," replied Linda. She was one of Evi's only friends these days. They hadn't met in person because Linda lived three time zones away. She was a beta tester, and the two of them had hit it off during the last upgrade of *Fields of Green*.

"He is? That's amazing," Evi said. Butter Bear had over two million followers on his stream, and he could make or break a game. The fact he had mentioned Evi's character was important, but that he loved the character was a once in a lifetime endorsement.

Evi had worked so many overtime hours that she could have a month's vacation. She watched the stream and let Linda babble on for a time. There had been so many challenges that it had been a relief to be done. Evi's inbox was dinging with people's congratulations.

Game design had been a difficult career path for her, not only as a woman but as a woman past her twenties. She had spent years consulting and providing IT for companies, and she wanted to do something different. Something fun. When she applied for the position, her mother said that she was nuts for quitting her corporate job. It was bad enough Evi wasn't married, but now she was giving up her secure job with a large company.

Evi was never one to follow convention, so she immediately put in her two weeks to begin the new position. She had been working hard to prove to herself she could create, and this was it. The warrior princess was a success. Take that, Mom! Heck—take that, world! Perhaps there would even be a bonus if sales were good.

Evi took a moment to glance at her texts. One of the messages caught her attention: *Hey Evi, I've been trying to call you, but it keeps going to voice mail. Can you call me when you have a minute?*

It was from Alex. Evi hoped it wasn't bad news. How could anything mess with this moment? She didn't want to ruin it. On the other hand, if it was news about Teddy, she wanted to know.

"Linda, I need to make a call. I'll get back on later, OK?"

"Yeah, that's fine. I want to log some time on *Fields of Green* anyway since everyone is playing it."

Evi ordered some food before calling Alex. "I hope it's not too late," she said when he picked up.

"No, not at all. I really appreciate you calling me back."

"I just saw your message, sorry. I was caught up because Butter Bear was saying how he loved playing my princess."

Alex chuckled. "There is a lot to unpack with what you just said, but I assume the butter thing is good?"

Evi laughed back. "Yes, it is a very good thing."

"I hate to have to share bad news while you're celebrating. I could call back?"

"No, it's fine. I assume it's about Teddy. Is he sicker? Is he in the hospital?"

The five-second pause answered her question.

"No. No, Alex . . ."

"I'm sorry, he passed a few days ago. From what I heard from the doctor, it was painless and quick."

Evi didn't do emotions. Her therapist was constantly telling her to stop trying to hold them in, but she couldn't let them out. Emotions only led to more anxiety, and anxiety was what kept her home in front of the screen even when she wasn't working. Her therapist had recommended everything from yoga to CBD, but nothing worked. Feeling emotions was too hard.

It felt like her heart had just been ripped out. Teddy, her college crush, was gone. Just like that. Instead of comforting a person she cared about, she had kept herself busy creating video games with her cat snuggled next to her. She was a monster. A monster that was now crying.

"Are you still there?" Alex asked.

"I'm a terrible human being. You told me that he was sick, and I should have been there for him. I am a monster. I—"

"Evi, you are not a monster. We all have lives and get busy. I'm as guilty as anyone."

"But you were there," Evi countered. "You were there when he needed you most. Me? I was more worried about my own anxieties and who would take care of my cat."

"I didn't tell you everything on our last call. So I'll confess now. When I first saw him, he was right outside the train station, standing there in the snow," Alex said. "To me, he was just another homeless man begging for money. I walked on by. I was too busy and wrapped up in my own head and ego. I walked right by him. I didn't want to be late to work."

"Really?"

"Yes, but I couldn't stop thinking about him all day. Then, the next day I stopped. I had to. Even then, I didn't want to be involved, and I knew I was getting into something bigger than I had time for. I had a big deal going on at work that I hoped would get me in with the partners, and I just didn't want to be involved. I would have rather given him a couple of hundred bucks to clear my conscience and move on. But I couldn't."

Evi got a notification from the delivery app. Her food had been dropped off at her door. She walked over, opened it, and picked up the bag. The grease from the burger and fries was staining the bottom. In her emotional state, it didn't look very appetizing, so she threw it on the counter and plopped on the couch. Captain was soon purring on her lap.

"What made you change your mind?" Evi asked.

"Sheri said a few things that were painful to hear. I was choosing to buy off someone who mattered in exchange for the possibility of becoming a partner. What really got me was realizing I could be him. When he said he didn't want to die alone, I could see myself becoming him. Teddy had no one else in the world. At least, that's what he was telling himself in his head. He needed me. A couple hundred bucks was not going to help Teddy. It wasn't going to resolve my feelings or change anything. Truth is, I needed him."

Evi stroked Captain and allowed herself to sniffle. She began to feel the depth and weight of her grief. The past was all coming back in strong, emotional waves.

They sat on the phone for several minutes, neither saying anything and both hearing background noises.

"So, is there going to be a funeral? Is there somewhere I can send flowers or make a donation?" She was doing it again—being a heartless monster. She had no intention of going to a funeral. Let alone the funeral of an almost ex-boyfriend. All the germs and that virus that was on the news. It sounded like a terrible idea, but at the same time, she knew she was putting up all these barriers to avoid the truth. She didn't want to be around people and show her emotions. She was uncomfortable enough crying in front of Captain.

"There's going to be a small service for the family, but there's going to be a memorial after that at Lake Geneva. Do you remember going to the cabin?"

"Yeah, that was my first and last encounter with Goldschläger." The thought of it assured Evi that the greasy bag on the counter would be in the trash after the call. Maybe a nice simple salad or some soup would be a better option.

"Before the family and others arrive, we can have the cabin for a few days."

"Who is we?" Evi asked.

"The group. Our group. This experience with Teddy has changed my priorities, Evi. I have neglected my family and friendships all in the pursuit of my career. I don't want to lose everything that's important to me. Our group got me through college. You guys were with me through the good and the bad, and being with all of you was one of the most important times in my life. I would love the chance to reconnect and start over. What do you say?"

What would she say? The idea of connecting with the group was wonderful. Traveling from LA to Wisconsin sounded terrifying.

"I don't know, Alex. And that's the most honest answer I can give you at the moment. I can take the time now, but I have . . . some personal issues I'm dealing with." She paused to give herself a moment to build the strength to be open. "You know, I talk to a therapist weekly, and she encourages me to get out in the world, but I don't even go to the store to buy groceries. It's an ordeal to go to her office, and recently she's allowed patients to video chat with her, which is wonderful. I have a lot of anxiety. Trust me, I want to go, but I just can't commit at the moment."

"I understand, and if you don't make it, no one will think ill of you. I'll send you an email with the details, and if you make it, well, it will be a really pleasant surprise. I'd love to have you there, Evi."

"Thank you. Thank you for saying that and for understanding, Alex," she said with sincerity. "If I can do it, I promise you I will."

After Evi hung up, she tossed the food. Just the smell of it made her stomach churn. Maybe she needed a change. Maybe it was time to step out of her comfort zone. She pulled on a hoodie and her Doc Martens, and she grabbed her messenger bag. It was time to go to the grocery store and buy some real, nourishing food for a change. It was the least she could do for herself right now.

EVERYONE IS AFRAID

Chapter 17:

CLOSING

"Peter Jacobson."

"Peter, it's Alex."

Peter's heart sank in his chest. Perhaps it was the tone of Alex's voice that tipped him off. "When did Teddy die?"

"Three days ago."

"Was he peaceful when he passed?" Peter didn't know why that was his first thought.

"He was."

"Was he alone?"

"With the exception of hospice, he was. It was in the middle of the night and I had left a couple hours before." Alex's voice conveyed a sense of sorrow and failure. "Teddy was alone when he passed. I'm sorry for not being there."

"Alex, please don't beat yourself up. Thank you for being

there for him and for not letting him be alone for the last weeks of his life."

As the words came out of his mouth, Peter felt a guilt that went beyond Teddy. It was then that he heard Justine's voice in his head: "Peter, I am OK that you weren't there when I died. The life we made together is what mattered to me." A wave of relief washed over Peter.

He and Alex were silent for several minutes. Both were being pulled between grief and gratitude.

Alex broke the silence. "There's going to be a small service for the family, but there's going to be a memorial after that at Lake Geneva. Do you remember going to the cabin?"

"Yes, I do."

"The group is going a few days early, before the family gets there. Peter, I'm going. I've invited Bhavani, Evi, Desiree, and now you. So far everyone is somewhere between 'that would be great' and reasons they can't. So far no one has said for certain no. Peter, I would love you to attend."

"Being busy has kept me from permanent drunkenness or worse," Peter replied. "Helping others find or sell houses has kept me sane and able to deal with Justine's death. I am not going to risk my thin grasp on survival by spending a few days thinking about the death of Teddy, or of Justine."

"I understand, Peter. May I call you occasionally? It's my commitment to stay connected to those I love."

"I would like that, Alex. Bye."

"Bye, Peter."

Chapter 18:

THE LAKE HOUSE

It was 2:00 p.m. and no one had arrived. No one had confirmed they were coming, and Alex didn't want to push. After sending each of them the information, there was nothing left but to wait.

He had arrived a few days before to make sure the house would be clean. A cleaning service had been there already, so the place was in decent shape. It had been vacuumed and dusted, and there were clean sheets on all of the beds. He went shopping for toilet paper, drinks, and the basics. Everything was ready.

The house was exactly as he remembered it. In fact, the decor had not been updated since the last time he was there. He enjoyed the nostalgic feel and it allowed him to step back in time and capture a moment when life seemed so much simpler. A time when he'd survived on ramen, cheap beer, and dreams of the future. As he passed by the large mirror in the vestibule, he stopped and wondered what had happened to that young guy who'd laughed and enjoyed time with his friends. Somewhere in those worn eyes was the young man who thought he would conquer the world. What had changed? It was the narrative that had changed—the one he had made up about himself. Was it possible to change that story?

Finding Teddy had made him want to rewrite his story. Since reconnecting with his old friend, Alex's marriage had improved some. He was up for a promotion, and he was feeling like part of a team for the first time. It seemed like everything was rolling, but how long would that last? How long before things either fell apart or slipped back into the old groove? And would there be anything he could do about it?

He remembered a conversation with Sheri.

"Why do you do that?" she had asked with her hands on her hips.

"Do what?"

"Why do you always assume the worst?"

He could rewrite that story. He could keep this change going.

A set of steps led off the wraparound porch onto the white sand. The pristine beach stretched forever in each direction. No one was around this time of year, and the lake was frozen. Alex squinted at the ice and could make out the glow on the horizon from Chicago's skyscrapers. During the summer, the group had gone down to the shore to play in the water and jump off the docks. At night, they would huddle around a bonfire.

The weather, while clear, was chilly, so there wouldn't be

EVERYONE IS AFRAID

any late-night strolls. There was no central heat or air in the home, but it did boast two large fireplaces and space heaters that Alex was pretty sure were a fire hazard with their exposed wire elements. As he was making sure all the rooms had extra blankets, the doorbell rang.

Alex opened the door to see a very tired-looking Bhavani. It was always a shock to see someone after so many years. As with Teddy, Alex's image of Bhavani had been fixed in time. In his mind, she was a pretty, athletic girl with her hair always in a tight bun. Once he adjusted, Alex could still see the girl behind the slight wrinkles and worry lines. And she still had the same bun.

"Bhavani," Alex said with a sigh. "You made it!"

A large smile crossed Bhavani's face. "It is so good to see you, Alex!" She dropped her bags and gave him a huge hug. It had been far too long, and Alex committed at that moment to not waiting until another funeral to see his friends. They had been so close that it was a shame they had lost touch.

"Can I help you with your bags?"

"Yes, that would be terrific," said Bhavani. "I am exhausted. I slept the whole way. There was a short layover in Denver, and can you believe I fell asleep and almost missed my flight?"

"Well, you can grab a nap," Alex offered. "The beds are all made, and I piled some extra blankets at the end of each one."

"I will take you up on that," said Bhavani. "I want to catch up, but it would be best for both of us if I get some rest first."

They reached her room, and Alex placed her bags on the luggage stand at the foot of the bed.

"Can I get you anything to drink?"

"I think I'll be fine. I'll just take a quick nap, thirty minutes max. I'll come down as soon as I wake up, I promise. And if you don't see me down there in the next thirty minutes, come knock on the door, please."

"No rush," Alex responded. "We have plenty of time."

· · · · · ·

The next to arrive was Evi.

"I'm sorry, Alex," she began before she even entered the house. "I tried to call your cell phone. You must think I am so rude for not confirming that I was coming. Did you get my calls? I should have left a message. But then I forgot and had to get a cat sitter for Captain and—"

"It's fine! Really," Alex replied. "It's my fault for not giving people the house number, but I didn't realize until I got here that there's no cell reception."

Evi's eyes grew to the size of full twin moons. "No cell reception? That's nuts. How do people stay sane? What happens if there's an emergency?"

Alex pointed at the phone on the wall in the kitchen. It was mustard yellow and had a long, twisted handset cord with a push-button keypad on the receiver. Alex picked it up so she could hear the buzz of the dial tone.

"You've got to be kidding?" said Evi with a look of horror on her face. She took a deep breath. "I guess a few days won't be too bad. At least I brought my laptop, so I can use it if I need to check on work or stream a movie. I hope the Wi-Fi isn't too slow."

Alex chuckled and shook his head.

EVERYONE IS AFRAID

"No. Alex, you're pulling my leg."

"This was a place to escape the world and unplug, remember? I was surprised the landline worked."

"What are we going to do?" replied Evi in a half-panicked voice.

"I suppose we will relax, talk, laugh, eat, and play board games, and I think there's a DVD player with some movies in the living room."

"No cable? What kind of house of horrors is this?" Evi stopped and took a quick breath. "I must sound so entitled right now. I'm sorry. We're here because of Teddy, and all I'm doing is thinking about myself and my needs. So sorry. Let me start over."

"It's OK. Seriously, you don't need to apologize. I am so happy you made it. Without all the regular distractions, we can catch up on literally *years* of missed time."

Evi cracked a grin. "If it includes some juicy gossip, I'm in."

. . . . . .

After Evi had settled in, she and Alex started going through old DVDs and laughing at how silly the movies were. Suddenly, there was a loud knock on the door. Whoever it was continued to knock hard until Alex could get to the door.

He almost laughed out loud. Desiree stood with a bag on each arm and a large roller suitcase.

"Uh, are you moving in Desiree?" Evi laughed. From Desiree's exasperated facial expression, she didn't appreciate the humor.

"What Evi meant to say is that it's great to see you, and can we help you with your bags?" Alex added.

"No, I got it," replied Desiree sharply. "Just point me in the direction of my room. It's freakin' freezing out here. I forgot the Midwest has real winters."

"Of course." Alex stepped aside to let her in. "The rooms are upstairs, remember? Take any that has an open door. You sure we can't help you?"

Alex felt bad as Desiree dragged her obviously heavy bags in. She was panting from the exertion. Evi had a point. She had brought a lot of stuff for just a few days.

"I got it, really. I didn't mean to be short. I just am not used to the cold anymore in sunny Arizona. It's great to see you two. Is Bhavani here?"

Alex had almost forgotten about Bhavani. "Yes, she's upstairs taking a nap, but I don't want to wake her yet. She looked exhausted. I think the sleep will do her good. I can't tell you how excited I am you all made it!" His grin was plastered on his face.

"Hey man, you called, and we answered," said Desiree, her tone a little more relaxed. "Let me get settled in, and then I'll come back downstairs and make margaritas so we can start toasting to Teddy."

"Oh, I just got some basics. I didn't want to get more until I knew who was coming," Alex admitted.

"Good thing I stopped off at the store on the way here!" replied Desiree. "I have more bags in the car."

"Oh, I'll get them," Evi offered.

"No, no, I got it," said Desiree. "I'll just be a minute."

She huffed her way up the stairs. Alex couldn't understand

why she wouldn't let them help her, but he had to remind himself that they were all virtually strangers. Sure they had a shared history, but that was a long time ago, and none of them really knew each other anymore. He hoped a few days without the regular distractions would allow them to get to know each other again—or anew. It was what Teddy would want them to do. Alex could feel the space Teddy had left behind. It would never be the same, but maybe they could learn from Teddy's life and be better.

EVERYONE IS AFRAID

Chapter 19:

REVELATIONS

The mixer was grinding ice, and Desiree was serving margaritas and making sure they had a salt-rimmed glass and a perfect lime wedge. She used red Solo cups for nostalgia purposes, but the drinks were perfect. As the group relaxed, Desiree served nachos, dips, salsa, and a plate of cheese.

"My goodness," Alex said. "You came prepared. Please let us help you."

"No, no," Desiree replied. "I've got this. You all sit and relax."

"Speaking of relaxing," interjected Evi. "Are you sure that we shouldn't wake up Bhavani?"

"I would let her rest. She seemed so tired when she walked in," Alex replied.

"She works at an ER, you said?" asked Desiree.

"Yeah, I can't imagine how crazy it must be with that strange virus appearing everywhere," Alex said. "Honestly, I'm shocked she made it."

"I'm shocked I made it," said Evi as she sipped her drink and speared a cube of cheese with a toothpick. "This isn't my thing. Do you remember me, guys? I wasn't Miss Social Butterfly. You were the only ones I really hung out with. Well, some things never change."

"Did you ever get married or have children? Not that you needed to," Alex said, catching himself in a statement that might seem judgmental.

"No, not ever really close. I have been seeing a guy on and off for a few years," replied Evi. "I'm just not the marrying type, I guess. Even though I enjoy our time together, he's never brought up marriage, so neither have I."

"Sounds like a loser to me," said Desiree.

Evi looked down at her lap.

"I don't mean to hurt your feelings," Desiree continued, "but you are attractive. In fact, I'm a bit jealous that you look as well as you do. I packed on a few pounds since college, but you look fantastic."

"No, I don't. I look old and plain," Evi replied.

"Are you kidding? Who told you that?" Desiree's hands were on her hips. "I know plenty of women who would die to have your figure, and you're brilliant to boot. Aren't you into computers now?"

"Yes, I'm a software engineer, but that just means I'm a nerd. No one could love a nerd who looks at code all day, plays video games, and is in love with Captain America."

They all chuckled at that a bit.

"I have to agree with Desiree," Alex said. "You have a lot to offer. You're smart and funny and have great taste in superheroes."

Evi smiled a little and then took another sip of her drink.

"So, do you want children?" Alex asked.

Evi looked into the fire crackling in the kitchen fireplace for a long moment, and Alex wasn't sure she'd heard him. He didn't want to disturb her thoughts if she was considering his question. Desiree frowned as she cut another lime and squeezed the juice with a reamer.

"You know, I do. I do want children and have even thought about adopting a child on my own. But I guess, if I'm to be honest, I really want to give birth to my own children. There isn't any physical reason I can't have a child."

"Does your boyfriend want a child?" Alex asked.

"I never wanted to push and ask. His parents divorced when he was young, so I just assume that he doesn't want children."

"Do you want to have children with him?"

Again there was a long pause as Evi stared into the fireplace.

"I guess . . . I don't know . . ." She trailed off, her eyes never leaving the fire. It was like she was in some sort of trance.

"If you want kids, then you need to find a good man to be a father," said Desiree. "Not so they'll help you around the house because God knows they're not much good for that—no offense, Alex."

"None taken." Alex chuckled.

"You need a man who makes you feel like you were struck by lightning and who will love your children. If you can't even talk to your boyfriend about kids, then how could he be the one?"

"I don't blame him for me not having children," said Evi as she broke from her trance and stabbed another block of cheese. "Especially with me. He knows I'm busy with work all the time and probably figures that I wouldn't be a very attentive mom."

"Did he say that to you?" asked Desiree, who was arranging a plate of cookies.

"No, but he probably thinks it, and he's probably right," said Evi as she nabbed a cookie.

"Do you believe that?" Alex asked.

"Well, not exactly. I don't know," mumbled Evi.

Alex could tell that she was becoming uncomfortable with the conversation, so he decided to shift the focus off her. Desiree's statements seemed a bit out of touch and out of date to Alex, but then Desiree was always one to speak her mind.

"Did you ever get married, Desiree?" Alex asked.

"Unfortunately, yes. But I couldn't count on Jerry for anything, so we divorced after two years. Irreconcilable differences."

"I'm sorry to hear that," Alex said with sincerity.

"Oh, don't be, Alex. He was supposed to partner with me in this coin-operated laundry business. I was always doing all the work, and he would never do what I asked him. But do you want to know the worst part?"

"What?" asked Evi. The frown was gone from her face, and she helped herself to a second cookie.

"We could barely make ends meet, and I thought the business was in the dumpster. So in the divorce, I just let him have it. I was sure he would be bankrupt in two months. Do you know that within a year, he had two more properties? And now, five years later, he owns over ten. I just don't get it. I was doing all the work, and we could barely stay afloat. I recently saw him at the grocery store getting out of a Beemer with his new arm candy. I feel played."

"So, he didn't succeed when you worked together, but after you got divorced, he expanded the business?" Alex thought he understood the picture Desiree was painting, but he knew she had to come to the realization on her own. He'd been the same way. If someone had said six months ago that he was the reason he wasn't moving up in the firm and his marriage was in trouble, he would have put up shields, dismissed the notion, and dismissed the person.

Desiree frowned a little as she thought. "Are you suggesting that I was the reason the business wasn't working?"

"Not suggesting anything," Alex replied. "I was more curious about what he did to make the business grow from one to ten."

"I don't know," Desiree said. "Maybe he had the ability to make it work all along but he was too lazy. As I said, I handled everything. He said he really didn't want to do tasks like emptying the money from the machines. He complained he wanted to do more in the marketing and financial aspects of the business, but he didn't have a degree in accounting or economics. He had a small business degree from a junior college. He just didn't have the knowledge I did, and he couldn't accept that."

"Oh," Alex said.

"You have a successful business now," Evi interjected. "I have a confession: I've followed you on social media. I saw that car you bought recently. I wish I had the money for something like that. But I'm not sure where I would drive in it. I don't go out much."

"Oh, that overrated piece of junk?" replied Desiree in a nervous tone. "I sold it."

"Why?" Evi's eyes went wide. "You looked so happy with that car."

"Yeah, I know, but I recently decided to simplify my life a bit. Consolidate. You know what I mean."

"But your business is doing well, right?" pressed Evi.

"It . . . has been a little slow lately. But this past week, we acquired this really big client. It saved us, and it allowed me to come here. Although I think I might need to go into town to check my email and make sure everything is going well."

"Who's running things while you're gone?" Alex asked. He finished his margarita and began heading to the sink with his cup and plate.

"I got that," said Desiree. "Just sit and relax. I got this. To answer your question, I have a business partner who's watching things while I'm gone."

"That's wonderful," Alex said. "You should be able to relax, then."

"She's great. But she doesn't know the staff like I do. Or at least I don't think she does. You have to keep on top of them and make sure they're doing a good job and that our company standards are being reflected."

"I understand," Alex said. "Especially with this new account. She may not know everything they're expecting."

Desiree got an odd expression on her face. "Actually, she landed that account, and so she knows what they want better than me. I just don't know if she can handle all the added staff and make sure everything runs smoothly."

"Have you ever left her in charge before?" Alex asked.

"Well . . . not like this."

Alex could see she was squirming a bit. "Maybe she can handle it, then," he suggested. "But I understand how you feel. I haven't taken time off in years. In fact, this past month, I had this huge account to prepare for, and then I had to decide whether to take the time and help Teddy or not. I really suffered, and I took a chance on another lawyer in the firm. He doesn't have my years of experience, and I was really worried we would lose the account, but I have to tell you—I was wrong. He nailed it. In fact, he did it better than I was planning to. My boss was impressed that I took a chance on him, and when I return after the memorial, they want to talk to me about being a partner."

"That's great news, Alex," said Evi. "Congratulations."

"That is fantastic, Alex," echoed Desiree. Alex could tell she was being genuine, but something behind her eyes told him she was distracted. Then Desiree chuckled. "Do you want any more margaritas? Last call!"

"I'm good," Alex said.

"I could use one last one," said Evi, holding up her cup.

"I'll join you," said Desiree as she began pouring tequila and lime juice into the blender.

There was a noise of opening and closing doors upstairs. Bhavani! Alex hoped she would come downstairs, even for just a little bit. But after a few minutes, when she didn't appear, he assumed she had just gone to the bathroom.

"So, what do you have planned for the memorial?" asked Evi.

"I don't know. I was hoping you guys would help me out," Alex replied.

"I was thinking maybe I could do a slideshow of his life?" Evi offered. "I have pictures of him and us from college. I found some pictures of him on the net, but it would be nice to have some more."

"You said you were in touch with his parents and his ex-wife, right Alex?" asked Desiree. "You could ask them."

Alex looked at the clock. It was 11:30 p.m. Too late to call them tonight.

"I could call them in the morning, and then we could go out for dinner. And if they want to email pictures, we could use the Wi-Fi in town. And you could check your business, Desiree."

They agreed it sounded like a great plan.

"I saw a drawer with menus from local restaurants. I can go through them and figure out a place to eat," said Desiree.

"That sounds great," replied Evi. "I am terrible at picking a place to eat. I'm sure you'll be much better at doing that than I am."

"Perhaps you could pick three good ones," Alex suggested. "And then we can put it up for a vote. We don't know what Bhavani might want, and I don't want to make a decision without her."

"I agree," said Desiree as she poured herself and Evi a drink.

"I hate to be a party pooper, but I am beat," Alex said. "So I leave it to you two ladies to keep the party going. Don't get too wild!"

Desiree smiled. "Ah, you know us!"

"Exactly, which is why I said don't get too wild." Alex laughed.

EVERYONE IS AFRAID

Chapter 20:

THE AWAKENING

Alex was usually an early riser, but someone was already in the kitchen when he made his way downstairs. There was the smell of strong coffee and bacon.

"Welcome back to the world of the living," Alex said.

Bhavani was sipping her coffee and looked a little startled.

"I'm sorry. I didn't mean to scare you," he apologized.

"No, it's fine. I was just deep in thought. There's plenty of coffee in the pot, and breakfast is on the way."

"I see," Alex said as he poured a cup.

"I have to admit I'm a little embarrassed," said Bhavani as she flipped the bacon sizzling on the griddle. On the counter were eggs, milk, juice, and what looked like a bowl of some sort of batter. She had clearly gone grocery shopping early that morning.

"Why are you embarrassed?"

"Because I slept like a hundred hours and missed everyone coming in. Why didn't you wake me?"

"I thought you needed the rest. You look a lot better this morning."

"Did I really look that bad?" asked Bhavini.

"You looked exhausted, not bad." Alex tried to be diplomatic. He didn't want to hurt her feelings.

"As you see, I got up at the crack of dawn and walked down the road until I had a signal, and then I got an Uber. We're in quite the dead zone here."

"You didn't have to do that. We were planning a trip to get some goods today."

"No problem. I got mostly breakfast items, as I didn't know what people wanted to eat later."

Alex grabbed some plates and silverware as Bhavani started to pour some pancake batter onto a hot pan.

"I guess I didn't realize how tired I was," Bhavani continued. "I guess a little time away from work was all I needed for my body to shut down. Once the caffeine and adrenaline were gone, I kind of collapsed."

"Does that happen to you often?" Alex asked. It reminded him a bit of his own mornings.

"No, because I'm always going. Especially lately. I've been doing double shifts."

"That must be hard. How come you've been working that many extra hours? The virus?"

Bhavani paused and plated the pancakes before answering. "Yep. So I have to. I'm needed at the ER. Recently we've been seeing more people with it. It's really bad. We have to wear a lot of extra protection. Getting in and out of that gear is a pain. It's been nuts."

"So are they short-staffed then?" Alex poured a second cup of coffee for himself.

"No . . . I just feel that they need me," replied Bhavani, but her tone betrayed that she wasn't confident in what she said.

"I can't imagine what it must be like working under that stress for that many hours. How did you get off work?"

"Well, they insisted. I didn't really want to take off, but my boss felt like I needed a break. I told her I didn't, but she insisted. So, since I had time to take off, I wanted to come and show my support."

"Where did all of this deliciousness come from?" asked Desiree as she and Evi entered the room in their PJs. The two women spied Bhavani at the same time and ran, and there was a hug fest.

"I wanted to surprise you guys," said Bhavani. "So I went to the store early. I figured I owed it to you since I slept through last night."

Evi filled her plate with bacon and pancakes and grabbed a glass of juice.

"You have no idea how long it's been since I was up early cooking breakfast," Bhavani admitted. "I kind of enjoy it!"

"Alex said you were really tired last night," said Evi before she bit into some crunchy bacon.

"Yeah, more than I thought I was."

"He said you're an ER doctor now?" asked Desiree. "I can imagine that being tiring."

"You have no idea. We have a medium-sized hospital, but it seems we're always at capacity. It is nonstop."

"Sounds like they need to hire more doctors," said Desiree.

"Well, not so much. We're adequately staffed. I volunteer for extra shifts."

Desiree just stared at Bhavani for a few moments. "Why?" she finally asked.

"Well . . . I'm needed. I'm very dedicated to the hospital, staff, and patients," replied Bhavani a little defensively.

"You just slept how many hours because of exhaustion?" asked Desiree.

"I . . . You know," replied Bhavani slowly, "you have a point. I was exhausted, and I just didn't realize it." She slumped against the cabinets. "I think I get what my boss was saying when she told me I needed a break. I was burning the candle at both ends." She slammed her fist on the counter. "I could have killed someone."

"What?" Alex responded in shock.

"Being that exhausted is dangerous. It impairs a person's decision-making. I could have killed someone by misdiagnosing them, giving them the wrong amount of medication, who knows."

"Oh, I see. But I don't think you'd ever kill someone," said Evi as she finished off another piece of bacon.

"That's the thing, though. In the ER, you have to make split-second decisions, and if your brain is not working at full capacity, you can make bad decisions."

"Perhaps, because you were tired, you were making bad decisions about working so many extra shifts," Evi offered.

"You're probably exactly right. How could I be so irresponsible?"

"I don't see it that way," Desiree said. "It sounds like you're trying to be super responsible."

"Tell me more," said Bhavani.

"You feel like they need you there and that you're saving lives. But does that mean you have to be there all the time? Every day? It sounds like you're committed to the care of others. That doesn't sound irresponsible."

"Yeah, but apparently I'm not taking care of myself."

"But you have a family, right? I'm sure you take care of them, right?" suggested Evi, filling her plate with bacon again.

Alex looked at Bhavani. Her expression seemed pained.

"I have some work to do when I get home," said Bhavani. "Time to give my life a much-needed enema."

"Oh, that's a nice visual." Desiree laughed. "Way to kill an appetite."

"You should see what I do every day right before lunch," Bhavani quipped back. "You'd never eat again."

"OK, OK, I get it," said Desiree. "I don't need any details. Listen, I can clean up here. You guys go relax."

"I can help," Alex offered.

"No, no, that's fine," said Desiree. "I got it. I have a particular way I like to clean a kitchen, so you go grab some coffee. I'll be finished here in no time."

"So, is Peter coming?" asked Bhavani.

"I meant to ask you that, too," added Evi.

"Well, I tried," said Alex. "Like the rest of us, he's extremely busy and has a lot going on in his life." Alex wanted to say more, but he wasn't sure it was his place to share personal details without Peter's permission.

"He knows the whole story, right? About Teddy not wanting to be alone and why we're all doing this now that he's gone?" asked Evi.

"Yeah. But I don't think he's coming. I sent him the details. I keep hoping he'll show up."

"Well, maybe there's still time," said Bhavani. "Peter was always on his own clock."

"Isn't that the truth," Alex said, and everyone laughed.

Chapter 21:

CAPTAIN

The group settled into the living room, and Alex started a fire. The wood that had been stacked was so old and dry it started right up. Desiree joined them with her own cup of coffee and a blanket.

"So, what's been going on with you, Evi?" asked Bhavani.

"Oh . . . you know . . ." said Evi as she twisted the hair that hung in her face around her finger. "I work at Space Rockers, a video game company. I'm a programmer for them. I work from home, which is great. And I have my little cat to keep me company. A cat is better than a boyfriend—she shares my bed every night, snuggles me all the time, even when I'm working, and she never complains and is never late for dinner."

"I have to be honest. I thought you would have ended up with Teddy," said Bhavani.

"Are you kidding?" Evi responded. "Alex mentioned something about that, but I can't believe it."

"It's true," said Bhavani. "He had the hots for you. He asked you out, and you turned him down."

"I don't remember it that way. Besides, we were all friends. It would have been weird."

"Would it? You didn't have the hots for him?" asked Desiree.

Evi squirmed in her seat, and her cheeks turned a bright rose color. "Who didn't? He would never have liked a geeky girl like me. It wouldn't have ever worked. Trust me. He was popular and good-looking. I was this mousy, shy girl."

"Did you miss the part where he asked you out?" replied Desiree. "I wanted to date him, but he wouldn't give me the time of day. He talked about you constantly. He couldn't figure out why you didn't like him."

"That's ridiculous. I just figured he was being nice because we were all friends. I didn't have many back in college. In fact, I don't have many now, but that's OK. My mom goes on and on about how I don't go out with friends or have any dates. I'm just fine with Captain Kirk, a glass of Chardonnay, and a good sci-fi series to binge-watch."

"Are you happy? I mean, truly content being alone?" Alex asked.

Evi paused and twisted her hair. "Happy is such a loaded word. Do I get lonely sometimes? Sure, I think everyone does."

Alex looked around the room, and he could see that there was agreement.

"I do feel alone," Desiree admitted. "I didn't realize how much until I began talking to you all and realizing how much I missed you. And how much I missed Teddy. He made me laugh a lot."

"Me too," added Bhavani. "He was a triple threat—handsome, funny, and smart."

"Even with all of that, he wasn't happy," Alex said. "His life was a mess, and he told me more than once that what he wanted most was to not die alone. I assured him I wasn't going away. I also made a promise to myself that I didn't want to die alone either."

"I worry about my cat," said Evi. She sounded a little choked up.

"Why, sweetie?" asked Desiree. "Is your cat sick?"

"No, she isn't sick. But I worry if something happened to me, who would take care of her? I had to board her to come here because my mom hates cats. I don't have real friends, and I don't have a boyfriend. Who would watch after her?"

"Oh, sweetie, don't fret. We got friends here. I could watch after your cat, what was her name, something Trekkie."

"Really?" Evi's eyes grew big.

"I could help, too, but there's no need to talk about it because no one else is going to die anytime soon. You hear?" said Bhavani.

"I . . . I guess, to be honest, it would be nice to have someone in my life. It's that guys don't like me, and they're intimidated by me."

"Did someone actually tell you that?" Alex asked.

"Well, no. Not exactly. I just know that's what guys think," replied Evi.

"I don't think that about you," Alex replied.

"You don't count. You're my friend, and you're married."

"I disagree. I do think it counts. I always thought you were cool and unique. I think you're making up stories in your head about what people are thinking."

"I don't think . . ." Evi began. "It's just that . . ."

Alex could see a conversation going on in Evi's head as she twisted her hair.

"Oh my gosh. Oh my *gosh*! Alex, you're right. Have I been doing this all along? Have I been pushing people away and not giving them a chance to like me?"

"I don't know," Alex replied. "You'll have to figure that out on your own. What I *can* say is that you have friends right here. And I think I can speak for everyone when I say we aren't going anywhere. I really don't want to lose any more of my friends or regret not seeing and talking to them. I've thought a lot about that day when I saw Teddy at the station. The odds seem staggering that we crossed paths, but I do feel it was for a reason. My short time with him has changed my life."

"I can say the same," added Bhavani. "I feel like such an idiot for not seeing the truth of my life. I spent all this time saving others and caring for them, but I was not taking care of myself. I promise you all that I am going to do better."

All eyes were on Desiree now.

"Oh, come on, guys. Of course this has changed my perspective. My issue has been about trust, and I almost lost my entire company because of it. My partner was there the whole time and was extremely competent. That's why I partnered with her in the first place. I seem to have forgotten that. I feel like I have to do everything, and if I let my guard down just a little bit, I will mess everything up. The only way to make sure I don't mess up is to be hyperfocused and never let myself relax."

Desiree sighed and looked at her friends. A tear rolled down her face. "I'm beginning to see my lack of trust in others is a lack of trust in myself. My fear of not being enough has me distrusting everyone. I didn't even allow you to help me carry up my luggage. Why did I bring so much stuff? I wouldn't let anyone help clean up the kitchen because my method is supposedly so great. I made you feel bad because I wouldn't let you help. Ah, crap, this is why my businesses keep failing."

"I don't care what anyone says. Everyone is afraid," Alex replied. "We are human, after all. We all feel that our flaws are something to hide and that we are required to figure things out on our own. I lived in this delusion—that asking for help is a bad thing, that admitting we're afraid or that we made an error is some sign of weakness. My life has shown me that my flaws are something I can own. I can share them and be open to help from others. Sharing them may be a good thing."

EVERYONE IS AFRAID

Chapter 22:

THE PLAN

The following day the cabin was a whirlwind as other guests arrived and Teddy's parents, wife, and kids settled in. The adults sipped cocktails, told stories of their day-to-day lives, shared pictures of their families and pets, and talked about Teddy. Most people left the same day, though Teddy's parents stayed overnight. In the morning, before leaving, Judy and Fred told Alex and the rest of the German club they were free to spend another night or as long as they wanted.

The group spent the final day relaxing and talking about college life, the professors and classmates they'd liked, and the ones that had driven them nuts. This was how Alex remembered the group, though back in college they'd had fewer worries about the worlds that awaited them at home. Still, today they were experiencing life in the moment, and it felt great.

"I didn't realize how much I missed Teddy until coming here. I can feel the loss. It's like I'm grieving Teddy but also grieving *us* and how much time we've lost," said Bhavani. "But at the same time, he's brought us together. I think he would be happy to see us having fun. Real *fun*. For the first time in a long time."

"I believe you're right," Alex said as he set the table for dinner. It was Evi's turn to cook; they had all drawn straws. She was a terrible cook in college, except for prepackaged ramen. She would cook a cup of ramen like a master chef. Tonight she was a little secretive about what she was making, but since this was their last night, she was going to use whatever ingredients were left. Everyone's fingers were crossed.

"You all have put so much of my life into perspective," said Desiree. "I really hate that this is our last night together."

"You know resolutions can be hard to keep without a plan," said Bhavani. "Just think of New Year's resolutions. Have you ever gone to a gym in the third week of January? It is a virtual graveyard."

"That is so true." Alex laughed.

"I've really valued our time and our discussions together," said Evi. "It's better than therapy, honestly. So why don't we commit to a group call once a month?"

Alex's first impulse was that he didn't have time. He would have work to make up and could imagine all the emails and documents that would be waiting for him. And then he stopped this train of thought and started a new one.

Time was what we made of it. That was the whole point, wasn't it? He needed to take time for things that were important.

He was in charge of his life. If talking with his friends was a priority, then he could carve out some time to do it.

"I can commit to that," he replied. "Let's do it on a video call."

Desiree looked up from her drink and said, "Listen, I feel like some kind of alcoholic these past couple of days—like I was trying to relive my glory days in college. But honestly, I have felt relaxed with you all. I know I need to make some changes in my life. My first thought was I don't have time, but then I thought about my mind shift just in the past twenty-four hours. I've decided I can't afford *not* to take time for a call."

"I'm in too," said Bhavani. "I want to keep my life on track, and I believe you guys can help me do that and keep me accountable to my promise to be different. I know I can't make all the changes I want to make overnight. It has taken me decades to become the person I am, so I can't expect everything to change right away. But I know that talking to you all can help me work on things one piece at a time."

Evi smiled and checked her watch. "So we're agreed. Excellent. And now . . . if you'll follow me to the kitchen . . . it's time for dinner."

When the group entered the kitchen, they saw a large bowl of salad on the table. There were all kinds of nuts and dried berries in it. It looked delicious.

Alex had smelled something roasting and hoped it would taste as good as its scent promised. "Wow, Evi. That looks wonderful," he said.

"I have a chicken and some roasted root vegetables. And dessert is a surprise."

"I am shocked," said Desiree. "This looks and smells edible."

"What is that supposed to mean?" asked Evi.

"I don't mean to hurt your feelings, but back in college, you tended to burn things. To a crisp."

"So you assumed I never learned to cook? I love to cook. I've taken a number of classes at the local chef's school. I don't know why, really, since I have no one to cook for except Captain Kirk. She loves my cooking. I make her these cat-friendly gourmet meals."

"That's amazing," said Bhavani. "I can't wait to dig in."

"Maybe I'll end up with more people to cook for. Maybe you'll all even let me cook for you again sometime. Maybe with our calls, you guys can help me with this bad habit of pushing people away and not giving them a chance."

"Hey, all we can do is listen and reflect what we see in you," Alex said.

"Exactly. That's what I think I need right now. The voice in my head has been very negative for a long time. Maybe my mom has been right."

"Oh, I don't know, sweetie," said Desiree with a wry smile. "I wouldn't go that far."

They enjoyed a laugh together.

The little group ate and talked about all the things they planned to do when they returned home. The energy in the room was high. Everyone anticipated the great conversations they would have in the future.

EVERYONE IS AFRAID

Chapter 23:

A YEAR LATER AT THE CABIN

"Where you off to?" asked Harriet as she handed Alex a coffee.

Instead of his regular messenger bag, he had a suitcase next to him.

"I'm off to see my friends for the weekend," Alex said. "I'm grabbing a cup of coffee while I wait for Sheri and the kids to get ready."

"Oh, that sounds like fun," she said.

"It'll be great to see everyone in person. I can't believe it's been a year since Teddy passed. It's been hard."

"I only saw you together for a short time, but it seems like he did have a profound influence on you."

"You think so?" Alex asked.

"You used to be so stressed and going all the time. But now, even though I'm sure you are busy, you seem more at ease. And I can't remember you ever mentioning a family vacation."

"That's because we haven't taken one in a long time. You're right. I have changed. I saw my reflection in him. I was going down a similar path. I didn't want to end up alone, so I made changes, and I keep making those changes."

"It's definitely obvious that you've changed," she said. "I've enjoyed our little chats in the morning even more than I used to."

"I have as well," Alex admitted. "It's funny. I used to rush to be the first person in and the last person out. I was always running and chasing. Now, I pace myself and take time when I need it. I actually get more work done, and people have noticed. I've been a junior partner for a year now, and I'm on the fast track to becoming a senior partner."

"That is excellent news," Harriet replied. "Can I say—you deserve it. You're a good man with a good heart."

Alex wasn't sure how to respond, so he looked deeply into his coffee.

"I have always known you were a good man," she continued. "I could see it in your eyes. I believe that now you have become that man I always saw locked inside you."

"I . . . Uh, thank you."

"Have you had breakfast?" she asked.

"No, we've been running around like crazy this morning."

"I will pack some sandwiches and snacks for your trip," Harriet said as she headed toward the fridge. "It's on me."

"Oh, I couldn't—" Alex began.

"I insist," she said. "My treat."

There was no use arguing. She bagged up the food.

As Alex waited, he got a text from Sheri: *We're almost ready. I'll meet you at the train station.*

He stopped at Harry's to grab a paper to read later.

"So good to see you," said Harry. "Are you going somewhere?"

"Yeah, the kids and I are going to a cabin for a few days."

"Oh, that sounds great."

"How are your wife and kids? Didn't your youngest just have a birthday?" Alex asked.

"Yeah, that's right. Good memory!"

Alex reached into the outside pocket of his suitcase and produced a small wrapped gift.

"You told me, and I wrote it down," Alex said with a grin. "You said he liked Pokémon cards, so I hope he likes these."

"Oh, no, no, this is too much," Harry said.

"It's not enough compared to what you give me every morning."

"What do you mean?"

"You always greet me with a smile, a good joke, and words to live by," Alex said. "You're one of the first people I meet in my day, and you help me begin it with a smile, so this gift for your son is just a small token of my appreciation. Not to mention you helped me bring a great new client to the firm . . ."

"Well, thank you, Alex. I know he'll love it."

They said their goodbyes just as Sheri and the kids arrived. She looked frazzled, and Alex helped her with one of the bags. He gave his wife a big hug, a kiss, and a smile.

"Off we go to our next adventure," Alex said as they headed toward the trains.

. . . . . .

"It was so nice of Fred and Judy to let us use this cabin again," said Bhavani. Kids ran through the living room, squealing with laughter.

"Slow it down, Lucy," Alex said, even though he was pretty sure he was being ignored.

"Don't worry," said Sheri. "Frank and I are taking the kids to a movie in town so you all can chat."

Sheri and Alex had become closer over the past year. Alex was spending more time with her, Steve, and Lucy, and he was a better man for it.

"You behave, Nelly," Bhavani said.

"Don't worry," said Frank. "She'll be just fine."

"You sure you don't mind going with them?" said Evi to her fiancé, George.

"No, not at all," George replied. "Besides, I better get used to it."

Evi plopped onto the sofa. Her baby bump was clearly showing.

"You sure didn't waste any time, did you?" asked Desiree. "I guess I'm the odd person out. No kids and no husband."

"Would you have it any other way?" Alex asked.

"Honestly, no. At least not right now. I've been too busy to mess around in love."

There was a knock on the door, and everyone was

EVERYONE IS AFRAID

surprised to see Peter standing in the doorway looking sheepish.

"I'm sorry I got lost," he said. "It's been a long time since I've been here, and the area looks so different."

Alex looked his friend over. Other than some wrinkles in the corners of his eyes and silver in his hair, he looked the same. Alex embraced him. Peter stiffened at first and then clapped Alex on the back.

"I'm so glad you're here," Alex said.

"I wasn't sure if I could do it. But I'm glad I did."

Bhavani saw Peter next, followed by Desiree and Evi. Everyone was squealing, and Peter still hadn't gotten through the door. His friends grabbed and hugged him.

"Give him some air," Alex said. "Let him get inside."

"You made it!" said Evi.

Peter rolled in his small bag, and Desiree grabbed his other bag.

"Like I was saying to Alex, I wasn't sure I was going to come. I felt really bad about ghosting you all last year, but I was in a really dark place. Alex convinced me—along with my therapist—that I should come. It was Alex's description of your calls and how close you've become that pushed me."

"We are so glad you came," Desiree replied. "And we'd love for you to join us on our calls."

Peter plopped down in a chair, his roller bag sitting next to him. "I guess I need to let you in on what's been going on with me."

"You just got here. Why don't you at least get settled in," Alex said.

"I . . . I believe I need to talk now, as I'm not sure I'll have the courage to later."

Peter described his wife's death and the drunk driver that had walked away from the accident.

"That's terrible," said Bhavani.

"This last year has been tough. Real tough. It wasn't long after I heard from Alex that I stopped caring. I told my broker I was done. She accepted it as a break. I continued seeing a therapist. Funny thing was I missed helping people buy and sell houses. Even though it felt so fake—transactional. These people weren't actually my friends. I became resolved that this was as good as my life was going to be. I wanted to continue that fake, boring, transactional life. Well, barely."

"I can't imagine how you're dealing with your loss," Alex replied.

"I believe my family and friends feel like I should get over it. Move on. I keep trying and failing. I don't think I'll ever get over Justine, but I'm learning to move through each day. Some days are better than others."

Everyone was silent for a few moments. No one dared to try to fill the space.

"I have also come to realize that I need—no, I want—other people. For most of my life, I have only counted on myself. I thought I needed to be strong all the time and that I could work everything out on my own, but I can't. And I need friends—real friends—in my life. So, when Alex talked about what you all were doing . . ."

Evi got up and gave Peter a huge hug.

"You are among friends, and we are so happy you're here."

Peter teared up a bit. And there was another moment of silence.

The landline rang and Sheri went to answer it. After she hung up, she returned to the group and said, "That was Julie. She and the kids are in town. They're going to meet us at the movie, and then we're all going out for pizza. So, you guys will be on your own for dinner."

"Not a problem," Alex said. He was overjoyed that Teddy's wife and kids had agreed to come. It was going to be quite a full house. There were cots and blow-up mattresses everywhere.

After the kids were off, the group uncorked a Rioja, and Evi settled for herbal tea.

Everyone had notebooks and pens. They had become very organized over the past year. They wanted to take notes, and they always recorded their sessions.

"I feel so underprepared," said Peter.

"Don't sweat it. We just like to record some of our thoughts," said Evi as she handed Peter a spare notebook and pen. "There is no obligation, but you might like to have it if you want to write something down."

"I can't believe it's been a year," said Bhavani. "So much has changed. And while it's been stressful at times, you all have been there for me every step of the way."

"Would you like to go first and sum up for Peter what you've been up to and those life changes?" Alex prompted.

"Sure," Bhavani said. "Well, as you know, this virus really ramped up, and the ER became overwhelmed quickly. I listened to you all and paced myself. No more double shifts, and I made sure I took time for myself, Frank, and the kids." She checked her notes and sighed before continuing. "I began training others on safety procedures to protect ourselves in the ER, and the hospital administrators noticed. They asked me to do a presentation. This led to changes across all the departments. More protective gear was supplied, and new policies were enacted."

The others were nodding, encouraging her to continue.

"They offered me the position of infectious disease coordinator for the hospital. It would mean a nine-to-five schedule and a bump in pay. My husband looked at me like I was nuts when I asked him if I should take it. To be honest, it was hard because I guess I had become kind of addicted to the adrenaline rush of the ER. But I found that it was going to be healthier for my family and me, and it was definitely in line with my career goals."

"You look so much more rested and peaceful," Alex said.

"You all helped me with that decision. Can you believe my husband and I went away for a week in the Caymans for our anniversary? A real vacation. It was bliss. We have a couple of other trips planned this year for the whole family. The *whole* family being a little bigger than it was, technically."

The group was puzzled, and then Desiree noticed that instead of wine, Bhavani had opted for herbal tea like Evi. She jumped up and hugged Bhavani. "Congratulations! Why didn't you say anything sooner?"

"We just saw the doctor before we came here, and he confirmed it. We haven't even chosen who we're going to tell yet."

"Do you know the sex yet?" asked Evi.

"No, it's too early. The trip to the Caymans was good!"

Everyone laughed.

"I guess I can go next," said Desiree. "I'm having twins!"

Everyone's jaws dropped. The room was silent.

"Oh, come on." She chuckled. "I'm not pregnant. I just felt left out. Are you having a baby, Alex?"

"Uh, not that I'm aware," Alex responded. "And thanks for that worry bug in my brain now. Anyway, what have you *actually* been up to?"

"You all know that when I returned from the memorial last year, I had a long talk with my business partner, Kate. I apologized for how much I had undervalued her and told her I was excited that she was along with me on this venture."

"How did she respond?" Alex asked.

"She cried. Then I cried. And then we got to work. Boy, have we grown this year. We've had to hire new staff and even some managers. Can you believe that? Kate suggested we step away from the day-to-day cleaning and have someone take over some of the roles in the business. She was right. We hired a marketing firm to help us as well."

"That is so awesome, Desiree," responded Bhavani with a huge smile. "So, what do you plan to do next?"

"I am so glad you asked that," said Desiree. "I have an announcement. I decided to sell my half of the business."

Minds were blown.

"Are you kidding?" Alex asked.

"This time, I'm not. What I realized is I don't really like the cleaning business. And because I don't have that passion, there is no way I could have grown the business this year without Kate. She's the one that has made all the big decisions and done the heavy lifting. She's been able to do this because I have given her the space to do it. I have trusted her implicitly, and it has paid off. I want to take the money from the payout and do something new and exciting. Something that I *am* passionate about. I've learned I want to be passionate about my life and my work. Working with someone as a partner is something I am passionate about. You have all taught me that."

"Do you know what it is you want to do?" Bhavani asked.

"I really don't right now. I'm still figuring it out, but I have also learned to listen to my heart, and when my heart tells me, I'll be ready. I still have some other investments, and I've downsized from my ridiculous lifestyle. Maybe I'll go walk the Camino de Santiago. That's something I've always wanted to do, and now I have the time to do it."

"I applaud you," Alex said. "It takes a lot of courage to do what you've done. What is the Camino de Santiago?"

"It's a pilgrimage in Europe. I remember last year you said that everyone is afraid, and you're right. Everyone is afraid. But we can be bold and surrender to being enough. We can face and confront that fear and keep moving. And that is exactly what I am doing."

The group congratulated Desiree and made her promise that when she went on her trip, she'd tell them all about it after.

"I guess I can go next," said Evi. "As you know, I found the love of my life, George. Once I realized that I was pushing people away, I was open to people coming into my life. We met at a cosplay meet and greet near where I live."

"Oh, I've heard about cosplay. What character did you dress as?" Bhavani asked.

"Uh, wouldn't you like to know?" Evi asked.

"Yes! I would."

"I'll show you pictures later. In private. I don't think the rest of you guys would see me the same."

Everyone chuckled.

"George is my everything. I didn't realize what I was missing in my life until I opened it up. It has been amazing, and I could kick myself for not doing it sooner. I know, I know. You're supposed to put the past behind you."

"I wouldn't be hard on yourself. We are, after all, human. We learn, and we grow," said Bhavani.

"I guess you're right," replied Evi. "It didn't take long before we were engaged, and of course, you know the rest of that story." Evi rubbed her belly.

"We need a plan for a baby shower," Bhavani said.

"Of course. And a wedding!" said Evi. "My newfound openness has also helped me in my career. One of the other developers wants to start his own gaming company. He had asked me before if I would come along, but the old me brushed it off. I thought he was just dreaming or maybe flirting with me. Neither of those things was true. He got some backers last month, and I agreed to join him. It's so exciting and scary at the same time. I'll be the creative director. I can create my own visions of games rather than working to develop someone else's. I really owe it all to you guys."

"You did the work," Alex remarked. "You earned it."

"You know, you're right. I did earn it."

Alex noticed that Evi no longer twisted her hair all the time. It wasn't too much shorter than it had been the year prior, but she seemed much more relaxed and less anxious.

He was about to go next when he remembered Peter, who had remained silent.

"Oh man, we've been a little insensitive with this talk of kids and families," said Alex.

"No, no. Don't apologize," replied Peter. "This is perfect. They say there's something like seven stages of grief, but I think I've been on an endless loop of stages two through four. I even became suicidal. Alex's monthly check-in got me close to that upward turn so many times. And now that I'm here . . . I want to be here."

Alex blushed but didn't interrupt Peter.

"I miss her every day. But I know Justine would want me to live—not just be alive. I wanted to reconnect with you all, and hearing your successes this year brings me hope."

Evi, who was crying, got up quietly and hugged Peter.

It was silent for another couple of minutes.

"I guess it's my turn," Alex said, and he cleared his throat. "I can't clearly express my feelings. Teddy saved my life. You all gave me a new life. A new sense of purpose and direction. Every month I look forward to our calls. I have learned so much about myself and have watched each of you grow. Again, my gratitude is beyond the words that I can muster."

There were grins all around.

"As you know, I did finally get my position as a partner at my firm. My decision to trust Todd to take over the big account was the best one I could have made. He not only secured that company, but it also led to referrals to even more companies who hired our firm. My duties have shifted some, but I am clocking out no later than five thirty most days. It's great to be home for dinner every night with my family. I've been able to go to dance recitals and meet with Lucy's teacher. She'd been struggling with math for a while, and I didn't even know it. I didn't let regret get me down. Instead, Lucy and I work every night on her math after dinner. Her grades have improved immensely."

"That's great news," replied Bhavani.

Alex continued. "And while Sheri and I are not having a baby right now, our relationship has improved tremendously. I hadn't realized how close our marriage was to ending. Now, it couldn't be stronger. Our conversations are real and more relevant. She's looking for somewhere to work. She hasn't resolved where, but it has to be someplace where people are having fun. And someplace where she can help others. Fourteen months ago I would have said life is OK. Why would we settle for OK?"

"I know what you mean," added Bhavani. "Things weren't good for me, either, but now, it's like we're on a honeymoon again."

The group continued to talk, share, laugh, and cry. The unspoken wish made by all was that wherever Teddy was, he could see he had brought his friends back together and that they had created this network, the benefits of which couldn't be measured.

Each person in the group still had their quirks, flaws, and misgivings. They still had fears and doubts, but because of their shared goal of support and understanding, they were able to overcome these self-imposed hurdles.

No matter how a person appears, everyone is afraid. The group no longer hid their fears; instead, they talked about them and chose to live their best lives.

Now, dear reader, it's your turn, and I believe in you.

EPILOGUE

Since you made it this far, I challenge you to go a little further. After listening to Dr. Jerko, I began a journey—more of a quest—to live a life where there was nothing wrong with being afraid. I chose to start by building a relationship with one person, then with several, whether I was afraid of them or not. This quest took me about ten years. From it, I created a methodology that worked well for me. People started saying I raised thought-provoking questions, and they'd ask, "How do you do that?"

I would tell them. And nothing would change for them. My scared self told me that just because something worked for me didn't mean it would work for anyone else. Telling others was impossible; I had proof it would make no difference. So I stopped trying to tell others and focused on taking care of myself. I did this so I could help Koni and together we could assist our family, Garrett, Lorin, and Brennan.

Later on, I was asked to speak to a group about networking. Panic set in. I knew what I was going to say, but my experience had shown me that whatever I said would make no difference. After speaking to the group, which made no difference, there was this story in my head: "Of course it made no difference. I had to discover it myself for it to work for me. They will have to discover it themselves for it to work for them."

That is what this book, our website, and our workshops are for. They are spaces for you to discover the same mechanics I discovered—but in weeks instead of years. Here's how to begin.

STEP 1: Be Your Stand

Your stand is the story in your head about what you will do, won't do, and might do. There is never a time when you are not being your stand. If you do something to help someone, that is your stand. If you do something to hurt someone, that is your stand. If you want to discover your current stand (yes, you have one already), look at what you will do, what you won't do, and what you might do.

Alex was living his stand when he was working long hours, not accepting help, and not being a part of his family's life. Think back to the story and see if you can notice each character's stand. They all have one, and many choose to change theirs. If it helps, make a list. Start with the college classmates.

Now take a shot at defining your stand: what you will do, won't do, and might do.

STEP 2: Care and Be Able to Give Help

Everyone has a lot going on. Most people are close to full capacity or a little beyond it. I know that when I'm over capacity and someone is telling me what to do, my defenses kick in. I shut the person down, and I feel like I'm not good enough. This is important insight. Just like me, everyone else is doing the best they can. Knowing this allows me to think about how to phrase something so that it doesn't feel like burden or a judgment.

For example, asking questions rooted in genuine curiosity can be helpful. It's better than asking questions only to lead people to a certain answer. Doing that is the same as telling them what to do, but it's less honest. Meet people where they are. Help them connect to the moment they're in, then move on to things they care about, like health, marriage/partnership, family, career, passions, and communities.

But if that goes down like a turd in the punch bowl, shift away from asking them questions and instead share a vulnerable story about yourself in a domain that could be relevant to them. Being vulnerable can allow the other person to lower their shield (the story in their head) and look at themselves honestly. It's kind of amazing. Being vulnerable is contagious—and it might even be a superpower.

Reflect on the story in this book. When were the characters telling themselves or others what to do? Which characters were asking questions or sharing vulnerable stories? Make a list of your favorite examples. Then try practicing vulnerability in the real world: share a story of your own and see what happens. At MacklinConnection, we call this "tossing lines."

STEP 3: Engage and Wait for the Imaginal Moment

Pay attention to what people say and look for openings. At MacklinConnection, we call these openings the imaginal moment. They are spots where you detect a person's story has shifted, has been reimagined, or is no longer useful. You can detect this based on body language and verbal cues.

Verbal cues might manifest as the person asking questions, challenging their own thinking, softening their tone, or questioning where you learned something. When someone lowers their defenses (by putting aside ideas like "I'm right," "You're wrong," "That never works," and "This is how it's done"), they might even get quiet. Either way, this means they're reflecting on their stories. Let them work through it. When they get to the other side and ask more questions, they are open to help.

Body language might manifest as someone dropping their shoulders or staring off into the distance. They might even get up and walk away. Let them go. When they come back, they will have a lot of questions.

Reflect on the book. Which characters had shifts in their stories? What caused it? Make a list. Then make a list of times in your life when your thinking shifted (like when I listened to Dr. Jerko). What was your old story and what was your new story? Can you share that with someone?

STEP 4: Share How We Can Help Each Other

You are not Master Yoda. Let me say that one more time: you are not Master Yoda. You are not teaching, and they are not your apprentice. Getting this wrong can make it seem like you're manipulating someone.

Be authentic and humble. You do not have all the answers. At best, you're looking for the questions—and you're looking for someone to find the questions with. This is how you connect. Share what you're working on and why. Maybe you're working to take care of yourself and your family.

Let them know you're a work in progress. Explain to them what you've tried and failed with, and what has worked for you. Ask what experiments you could design together. Go and run those experiments.

In the book, who was being humble and looking to build connections? Make a list. Were those characters likable? Would you like to hang out with them? Now make a list of people you can connect with in the search for questions. Write down what you can share from your own journey—what has worked and what hasn't.

STEP 5: Provide Options to Connect

Inviting someone you're building a relationship with to connect further is a sign of trust and belief. You could be in a class, a workshop, or the workplace. You might be talking to a vendor, a customer, or someone joining your team. Offer them the option to connect. It doesn't need to be significant—just a pathway to continue dialogue.

In the book, who invites others to connect? How did they do this? Was it high pressure? Was it seductive? Was it clear that the character would still value the other person even if that person declined to connect? How can you offer connection in your daily life?

STEP 6: Allow Others to Accept Connection

Be patient. Being patient is underrated. Once you start building a relationship with someone, you'll be tempted to rush the connection. This makes it about you, not them. They have busy lives, many commitments, and lots of stories going on in their heads.

You may decide they're avoiding connecting with you. That is a story about you. If you're frustrated, reread steps 1 and 2 of this epilogue.

Be open to the fact that it may take hours, months, or years for someone to be ready to connect. It is their choice. Be your stand.

In the book, who was anxious and who was patient? Make a list. Reflect on times when you've rushed connections. How would you do things differently now?

STEP 7: Allow Others to Contribute to You

It's great when someone wants to help us, right? This is an important step, but it can be the most uncomfortable. Accepting help requires vulnerability. When others decline your help, how does that feel? Do you feel more or less connected? When someone lets you help them, how does that feel?

Reflect on the characters in the book. Which ones would not accept help? Which would? How did you feel about them? How did they make other characters feel about them? Which characters began to accept help? What difference did that make in their lives?

Rate yourself on your ability to accept help from others. Do you treasure the help and the connection you're building? Or do you feel uncomfortable and obligated?

· · · · · ·

These seven steps can increase your capacity to build professional and personal connections. They are the foundation of our methodology at MacklinConnection, and we offer workshops at ImaginalCommunity.mn.co to guide you. Why did it take me ten years to assemble a methodology that works? That's a long story, and maybe it'll be a future book titled *Everyone Is Now Uncomfortable: An Introvert's Guide to Bludgeoning Others with Good Intentions.*

You might have a story in your head about me being unapproachable because I wrote this book, I created the Macklin Method, or you've watched some of my videos. But I promise you, I will be honored to hear from you. You can find me on LinkedIn, send me a text or email, or sign up at ImaginalCommunity. mn.co. Send me a chat there. Let's connect.

ACKNOWLEDGMENTS

For the making of this book: Dan, John, Deb, Joanne and Michelle

For the making of the stories this book is made from: Harley and Sandra, Kathy, Lorin and Vleda, Koni, Dan, Mike, Mark, Wes, Steve, Jun and Billie, William, Jim, James, Karen, Mike, Fred, George and June, Jerry, Dianne, Ron, Jim, Ray, Dave, Carl, Steve, Allen, Ben, Vince, Tim, Petra, Frank, Berndt, Holger, Wade, Shannon, Mike, Billy, Don, Doug, Beth, Val, Tom, Craig, John, Greg, Andre, Nicole, Warburg, Kathleen, John, Karen, Al, Mike, Eric, Eric, Angelia, Thomas, Elaine, Toby, Linda, Jeannie, Greg, Read, Ann, Bruce, Susan, Ivan, Tanmoy, Dave, Rhett, Scott, Nick, Bev, and Monty. If I forgot someone, please forgive my memory, you all live in my heart.

For those who were my purpose for making me who I am today: Koni, Our Marriage, Garrett, Lorin and Brennan.

And for those who believed in me, especially when I did not, you know who you are. Your belief alone created a better world. Thank you.

And for those who didn't believe in me, you also know who you are. Thank you, I love doing what others say can't be done.

And to God, thanks for all the opportunities for me to get ready for what's next.

ABOUT THE AUTHOR

Ron realized early in his engineering career that he had a passion for building and leading teams. And he realized that to succeed, he needed to build a deep network of support. He needed to learn why people connect and how they create results together. This realization led him on a 20-year journey that culminated in the creation of the 7-step The MacklinConnection Method and the launch of MacklinConnection. Ron earned a degree in engineering from Kansas State University and quickly grew into leadership positions in his career. Ron grew to lead teams that set nine world records and won dozens of customer satisfaction awards. At Siemens, for example, Ron led a support division with 350 employees that worked over 5 million hours without a lost-time injury and was voted "the best place to work in Houston" by the Houston Business Journal. Twice Ron has created a growth culture responsible for increasing profits by $20 million, and has led seven different groups from worst- to best-in-class. Today, Ron is the president of MacklinConnection, overseeing our programs and extending the reach of the organization worldwide. He continues to lead programs and coach teams and individuals. A Wichita, Kansas native, Ron and his wife Koni have three adult children, Garrett, Lorin and Brennan.

CAN YOU HELP?

Thank You For Reading My Book!

I really appreciate all of your feedback, and I love hearing what you have to say.

I need your input to make the next version of this book and my future books better.

Please leave me an honest review on Amazon letting me know what you thought of the book.

Thanks so much!

. . . . . .

www.ingramcontent.com/pod-product-compliance
Lightning Source LLC
LaVergne TN
LVHW052023080426

835513LV00018B/2130